14.44

METTA MOM

A Mindful Guide to Managing Your Mood & Your Brood

By Vanessa Linsey

For Mom.

Contents

Contents

"People fear miracles because they fear being changed—though ignoring them will change you also. Swede said another thing, too, and it rang in me like a bell: No miracle happens without a witness. Someone to declare, Here's what I saw. Here's how it went. Make of it what you will."

- Leif Enger, *Peace like a River*

1986

Two days after Christmas, my sisters and I are still coming down from our collective holiday high. We spend the morning finding quiet corners of our cozy farm-town home to remove tags from clothes, read new books, polish nails, and extract the last bits of chocolate from our homemade stockings.

I am 11 years old, the baby of the family, and rely heavily on my sisters for entertainment. After a couple of hours alone, I decide it's time to start bugging the bigs.

Monopoly?

Othello?

No takers.

I bounce into the kitchen and find my mother doing dishes, "When's Pop coming home? I wanna play a game," I chirp. Without meeting my eyes, she tells me she isn't sure when he'll be back from Grandma's.

An occasional overnight at Grandma's house is not out of the ordinary, but Mom's half answer tweaks my Spidey senses. I march myself directly to the powder blue rotary phone in the living room and spin out Gram's number. Pop picks up quickly, and I quiz him on exactly what time he will be home because I am desperate for a game of Monopoly and all of the people in this house are BOR-ING.

"Put your mother on the phone," he replies.

An hour passes. Mom calls my oldest sister to her bedroom for a private talk. *Hmmmm... mysterious.* The pair disappear behind her thin particle board door, and I cleverly place a glass against it to eavesdrop. The glass does not work. Come to think of it, the glass never works. I lie down on the nubby gold hallway carpet, nose to the crack under the door, and wait. When my sister emerges, I shoot up, wiping drool off my cheek and rubbing my eyes.

"Wanna play—" I start.

She side-eyes me a look of disgust as she crosses briskly to her bedroom. She slams the door behind her as my mother calls out to sister number two.

It's another hour later; another sister skulks past me in tears. Mom peeks at me from behind her door. Her face looks tired, her eyes sad.

"Vanessa?" she beckons. I guess I can forget about family game night.

"Where's Pop?" I ask again, this time not so enthusiastically.

She gently closes the door and explains that he is at Grandma's and he is not coming back. I know it is all my fault because I was the one who called him that afternoon. *How could I be so stupid? If I hadn't called him this would not be happening. I would not be sitting here, picking lint balls off my mother's white cotton bedspread, listening to her tell me that my father is gone forever.*

I leave Mom's bedroom, walk slowly around the house, notice now-obvious clues I'd overlooked a few hours earlier. Pop's clothes are gone, as are his guitar, our olive-green Jetta, my pink hairbrush that he's always stealing, and the ubiquitous smell of marijuana. But he has left something behind that will grow with me over a lifetime: his pain.

Lovely. A hairy beast of my very own.

Introduction

Metta

Did you know that if you place two guitars on opposite sides of a room and pluck the six-string on one, the six-string on the other vibrates? Neat, right? It's because the un-plucked string naturally seeks the higher vibration. In the same way, when a peace seeker strums their heartstrings, those around them attune to meet their vibration. One person's peace practice could easily affect a hundred people or more.

Metta is a type of Buddhist prayer that is not only a beautiful way to strum those heart strings, but also sums up why mindfulness and meditation are vital practices, as one person's wholesome efforts stimulate collective healing.

A Pali word meaning "loving kindness or friendship," Metta is the single love drop that inspires a tiny love ripple that eventually turns into a powerful love wave. In practice, a Metta prayer is directed first at oneself, then to a benefactor, then a non-romantic loved one, a neutral person, a challenging person, and finally to any being who is home to a soul. Metta A classic example of Metta is: *May I be happy. May you be happy. May they be happy. May we be happy.* Each chapter in *Metta Mom* begins with a Metta prayer inspired by the stories that follow.

Metta Mom is organized into three parts: *First You; Then Your Family; Then... Whole World* (so meta). Beginning with you, the single love drop, *First You* explores ways to link daily drama to hidden trauma so that you can reduce stress, increase creativity, think in solutions, heal relationships, forgive self and others, and even spark joy. Threaded throughout this section, you'll find tips for nurturing an insight practice while managing depression, temper tantrums, setbacks, and more. While there are plenty of references to parenting and families in this opening section, *First You* is more about strengthening your own emotional foundation.

In part two, *Then Your Family,* a love ripple starts to quiver. Once you get a good handle on challenges and triggers that drive your behavior, you discover space to explore mindful parenting strategies that help you maintain your personal integrity while living with people whose agendas are at times in opposition to your own. Your family's energetic vibration naturally pulses in frequency with yours; during those times when it doesn't, you don't get sucked into a whirlpool.

The final section, *Then... Whole World,* reads differently than the first two sections. In it, I detail some of my own examples of divine guidance and synchronicity, so you can see how my spiritual ascension process materializes. Part three demonstrates how engaging spiritually based mental health practices over time generates a love wave that delivers beneficial relationships, resources, and outcomes. The force and magnitude of this wave urges you to wake to a profound understanding of self and others, to embodiment of your divine cosmic nature, and to a shift in world view from otherness to oneness.

Instructions

Within the pages of this book, you'll find ideas that support emotional and spiritual ascension. Emotional ascension lifts you out of your conditioned way of reacting to and recovering from human experiences. We ascend emotionally by reconciling the past.

Spiritual ascension opens your awareness to a divine way of seeing and relating to the world. We ascend spiritually by surrendering to the present.

If you choose to use *Metta Mom* as an ascension tool, you may be surprised by the ways this book works into your life. Throughout the last decade of devouring self-help books[1] and spiritual teachings, I have noticed a consistent trend: each time I read a powerful lesson or workshop with a new teacher, the Universe immediately provides an opportunity to work it through in real time. *Metta Mom*'s stories may trigger tricky situations for you, too, in which case you will need a few days to notice, reconcile, and transmute those emotions.

With that in mind, I suggest reading *Metta Mom* slowly. Read one chapter, then put the book down. **Let each lesson run its course in your mind and body before moving onto the next.** During that time, test drive mindfulness approaches that can help you navigate challenging experiences and give yourself time to see which of them work. If you begin to dredge up emotional trauma or physical pain that feels super intense, please seek professional help.[2]

Healing via mindfulness and meditation begins with everyday experiences—while walking the dog, riding in an elevator, filling the gas tank, or checking email. In the same way we use Metta to love ourselves before learning to love those who challenge us, we practice mindfulness in *moments* that we love before practicing in *moments* that challenge us.

In Montessori school in the 1970s, we were taught to clean up a spill before we were taught to pour water. I remember learning this

---

[1] See the partial list of titles that have influenced my journey and that complement *Metta Mom* teachings at the end of this book.

[2] If your needs are less therapy and more support, form a *Metta Mom* book group and work through one chapter a week together. Lean into your Sisterhood. That's what we're here for.

lesson when I was about four years old, squatting on the schoolhouse floor, filled with curiosity and responsibility as a deliberately placed puddle shrank into my dry sponge. When the day came that I began pouring water from a small glass pitcher into a tiny glass cup, I was prepared when water spilled on the floor and didn't panic. I used my Montessori training to quickly retrieve a sponge and clean up the mess.

A strong mindfulness practice is developed in a similar fashion. By developing insight during uncomplicated times, we're better equipped to flourish in the messy ones. If you start mindfully observing yourself for the first time while you're sick with strep throat or in a wicked fight with your teenager, you'll be turned off from the practice. So don't do that. Wait until you're relatively comfortable before trying a new meditation practice, or even diving into this book.

At the end of each chapter, there are journaling prompts to assist you in your healing and inspire you to record insights. **It is imperative that you record your healing journey because measuring your progress validates your hard work and reinforces the learning.** This could be done in a journal, blog, or video diary. Think of yourself as a scientist, keeping detailed notes on every observation you make as you seek your Truth. Don't waste this healing effort by being slack about keeping track.

One more thing about *Metta Mom*: I swear in it. I like to use the word shit, especially when I write. It might be because I think potty talk is funny, which could make me come across as highly un-evolved. I'm okay with this for two reasons: one, I am a work-in-progress; and two, even though I meditate and practice mindfulness, my personality is still fully intact. I still have quirks and opinions and style and edge. And I still like to swear.

It's funny—about a year into my practice, I started hoping that meditating would make me cool. Not cool like Danny Zuko, but cool like your favorite yoga teacher who is kind of out there but can still balance a checkbook and eat the occasional Oreo. (You know the one.) Anyway, that didn't happen. I'm still a spaz. Many years into my formal practice, I accept my un-coolness, having decided to no longer berate it or defend it or try to change it. In *Metta Mom,* I hope you find ways to light your own path toward un-coolness, acceptance, forgiveness, healing, joy, love, connection... all that and more.

Part 1

FIRST YOU

1

May I dig deep. May you dig deep. May we dig deep.

Hahaha

Years ago, I saw His Holiness the Dalai Lama at an event in Boston. He spoke to us about cultivating peace, then pointed one thick, straight finger at the audience and urged, "First you. Then your family. Then your neighbor. Then... *whole world!* Hahaha."

I laughed with him. He was cute. He was a highly evolved world leader, but he was also adorable. I don't think he'd mind my saying so. His ability to waggle a finger commandingly at thousands, then immediately surrender to a full belly laugh, can only mean he doesn't take himself too seriously.

Relaxing into my seat with a wide smile, I appreciated his playful delivery and understood why the Dalai Lama cannot have children of his own—he has us. From stage, he represented the enlightened Father, and we his brood of unruly kids. His job that day was to deliver a desperately needed lecture without us tuning out or walking out.

For me, his lecture resulted in a feeling of potent urgency and dulcet ease. I realized in that moment that this is how I want to parent my own kids: so that they know I mean business, but they also know I have ready access to forgiveness and joy.

Forgiveness and joy do not always flow freely, especially while getting verbally clobbered by a budding teen for kissing her goodbye at the bus stop or busting a toddler doodling on wallpaper in black Sharpie. If too much of the *yuck*—depression, relationship drama, habitual negativity, emotional insecurity, anxiety, and so forth—clutters the brain, there's no space for forgiveness and joy to work through us. In order to function effectively at the intersection of discipline and levity, it's necessary to free up some mental real estate.

Parental badassery requires the Dalai Lama's "first you" action plan: If you're in your right mind, the rest of the family has a fighting chance. You offer your children a better you; they, in turn, pay it forward, offering the world a better them.

My "better me" is far from perfection. I still feed my kids cereal for dinner, pay my Visa bill late, and ignore perfectly foldable mountains of clean laundry, but I don't let these conditions fool me into thinking I'm a bad person, much less a bad parent.

Still, I know all too well what it's like to think I'm a bad person. For most of my adolescence and young adulthood, I believed myself to be a worthless, unlovable throw-away. Happy moments were tainted by a burdensome beast. You know this hairy mongrel. He's the one that started loitering under your bed after that second grader called you fat. He's the stinker that snuggled up to you every time your dad lost his job, your mom drained a martini, or your big brother kicked your ass. Maybe you saw your hairy beast every time you looked in the mirror—wishing your tummy flatter, your hair straighter, your skin clearer. Maybe your beast is like mine—the daddy-less daughter kind, reminding you that you are small, inconsequential, disposable. He loves pinning you down in your yuck. And once the beast shrouds you in filth, you pass your ratty old hair shirt on to your kids.

At least I do.

Rather, I did.

When parenting from the yuck, I'd punish my kids for being silly at inappropriate times, for not eating dinner, for making messes and not cleaning up. I'd micromanage their friendships, their words, and their behaviors. My mind was in a perpetual state of judgment and criticism.

When I discovered *mindfulness,* the intentional and compassionate observation of thoughts, emotions, and physical sensations that holds your attention in the present moment, my yuck started to decongest and many of the less impressive aspects of my parenting practice broke up along with it. I mindfully tapped into some of that levity demonstrated by the Dalai Lama and realized I was trying too hard to control my kids. I needed to be more discerning about the moments I chose to bring the hammer down and allow more space for laughter and silliness. They are kids, after all.

This mindfulness journey began for me over ten years ago, casually at first. I didn't know what an enormous, positive effect mindfulness would have on my life (which is good, because if I had known that this practice would teach me to like myself—even love myself—I'd have quit).

Mindfulness heightened my awareness. I began to catch myself wallowing in hand-me-down yuck, and eventually noticed when I was dumping that yuck onto my kids—and I wanted to course correct quickly.

I became infinitely more flexible and forgiving with my kids. Spilled the nail polish? Cracked the iPad? Crashed the car? We'll figure out how to get through it. (My kids have done all of these things and will testify that I've responded with total composure, thanks to my practice.)

When our children see us respond to drama with forgiveness and solutions rather than blame and reactive punishment, they have a better chance of doing the same.

Here's the rub: Reading a book on mindful parenting isn't going to make you a mindful parent. You have to practice mindfulness to be mindful.

Like, daily.

I know. You're busy. And it's hard. But it's not as hard as a year in the slammer, six rounds of chemo, or life under communist rule. Really, the only hard thing about practicing mindfulness is remembering to practice mindfulness.

Reading this book means that you and I are now officially in this thing together, so let's make a deal. I promise to remember to be mindful every day—whether that means sitting in formal meditation for 30 minutes, communicating mindfully with my colleagues, or surrendering completely to a game of *Settlers of Catan* with my kids. You, in turn, promise to give the practices in *Metta Mom* a shot.

Triggers

Michael and I have four kids. Chelsea leads the pack at age 27. She eased me into parenthood 16 years ago when I became her stepmother. Our younger set includes Penelope, Scarlett, and Xavier—currently ages 14, almost 13, and 10. I love these youngsters fiercely, with all my heart. They have catalyzed my healing and ascension journey just by being alive.

For a long time, my emotional composure was dependent on my kids' behavior. When they were walking on sunshine and rainbows, I was walking on sunshine and rainbows. When they were spiraling in flames toward the earth at top speed, I was spiraling in flames toward the earth at top speed. We spent more time looking down than up.

Years back, while hovering piteously (and regularly) over the mangled wreckage of toddler tantrums, I began to wonder if all this crashing and burning was normal. It seemed to me that most parents endured manic kid drama, but did we have to be swallowed up by it? Was there a way to unstick myself from this cycle? Could I somehow scooch my family forward on the emotional teeter-totter and enjoy the relative balance of the fulcrum?

In attempt to evolve into a centered and happy parent, I read dozens (and dozens) of parenting books. I learned 257 different ways to soothe my baby, discipline my child, and stepmother a tween. My dog-eared, sticky-note-covered paperbacks were jam-packed with neat pairs of hypothetical problems and researched solutions: *When your baby cries, swaddle him like this. Never let your toddler watch TV. Family dinner is the key to your child's success. Your daughter's obsessive perfectionism is a gift. Your son's ADHD is a gift. Your teen's rebellion is a gift.*

Some of these texts helped me survive parenting crises, like bed wetting and separation anxiety; but when it came to managing drama that blocked my access to happiness on a daily basis, I enthusiastically implemented these authors' ideas for a few weeks (okay, okay, *days,* a few *days*), then retreated to my old, familiar, grimace-y ways. Unlike other moms I knew, I could never "best practice" my way to feeling good about my parenting, and I assumed I was doomed to ruin my kids.

The reason parenting books did not and could not provide me with emotional composure or sustainable happiness, was that my sadness and bewilderment were rooted *not* in parenting, but in my own childhood trauma. Without realizing it, my long buried, barely visible yet ever-present pain was triggered easily and often by people and circumstances surrounding me. I call these *topsoil triggers*: mundane interactions that actually drive us a little berserk.

Example: one day I was taking a walk and noticed a stream of friends arriving at a neighbor's house for a party that I had not been invited to. The exclusion stung. Because I have a deeply rooted experience in abandonment (rejection and exclusion are lumped into this category for me), this social slight caused my mind to slip down the rabbit hole. I assumed fault for the brush-off, tried to remember conversations in which I could have offended the host, and wondered if she didn't like me. I imagined multiple narratives around the snub, then brought the stories to life by talking about it with a friend. My friend felt angry on my behalf and agreed that I was unfairly treated. She scratched a deeply rooted itch for me, unknowingly confirming the abandoned child story I'd been playing on repeat in my head since I was 11 years old.

By acknowledging that our topsoil triggers have roots, we clear the first hurdle that looms between us and our much-deserved emotional composure. Other hurdles appear quickly, though, as we're uprooting these triggers under the duress of parenting. The lack of sleep, the absence of control, the physical demands, the financial drain, the time crunch, the constant sound of our own nagging voice… it all makes us feel tweaked to begin with. Filter these parenting conditions through our childhood trauma *and* toss in a few little people who look just like we did when we experienced the trauma, and we might be tempted to believe it's easier to stay tweaked.

It's true, we can't change these conditions, but we can have compassion for ourselves during humbling times when we make shitty parenting choices.

Hey! That's great! We've already made progress by bringing awareness to the fact that detangling from daily drama may require some excavation into our past and acknowledging that it won't be easy to do this while dripping with children.

Friend, we are absolutely capable of creating a new narrative.

Instead of weaving stories based on assumptions and habits, we can affirm joy-centric narratives that are in alignment with our desired emotional and spiritual integrity.

The topsoil story I shared concluded quietly. My name was omitted from the guest list by accident. *Oops!* The party host called me a week later and apologized, but not in time to stop the thought train from chugging toward destination Loserville. I'd already spent seven days stuck obsessing, seven days stuck distracted, seven days stuck pumping out bad vibes, seven days stuck creating new problems.

I'd also spent seven days gossiping on the phone with little ears nearby, seven days avoiding interactions between my kids and her kids, seven days preoccupied by runaway thoughts instead of focused on my children's needs, and seven days parenting my babies through the lens of a loser mom.

That social drama revealed a dozen habitual pitfalls. The hardest lesson to take: my internal chaos is a sucker punch directed right at my kids.

We can call out and intellectualize these changes in mindset with relative ease, but to embody them, to allow them to seep into our life, body, interactions, and very way of being, requires an intentional willingness to heal, a real desire to be happy, and a good old-fashioned college try.

Chapter Summary:

May I dig deep. May you dig deep. May we dig deep.

Old trauma may be very easy to pinpoint, though hard to connect to the destructive things we do today. Old trauma can also be subtle—moving homes multiple times, being called stupid by a sibling, or witnessing an accident—making it hard to identify, but nonetheless destructive over the course of a lifetime. This first chapter should remind you of several things: 1) Freedom from trauma is your divine right; 2) your past, which may have been quite unruly, informs your present conditions; 3) the work you do in the present informs your future; 4) it's not too late to be free—but you'll likely have to do a little digging first; 5) you are equipped with the tools you need to heal yourself.

Journal Prompts:

- Do you have any topsoil trigger stories in your life? Just one? Many?
- Everyone suffers. Everyone gets triggered. Do you know what your habitual triggers are? Who really knows how to get under your skin? Where do they land in your body? How do interactions with this person make you feel?
- How have you dealt with triggers in the past? What's worked for you? What hasn't?
- Do you sometimes take your kids' antics too seriously? Do you have one kid who really presses your buttons? Why? What would happen if you just laugh with them? Try it. Write down what happens.

2

May I be unstuck. May you be unstuck. May we be unstuck.

Beast

My hairy beast sucked.

He told me I was worthless. He spoke out of turn. He wedged himself between me and the things I wanted. He broke up relationships; he hurt my friends and family. None of this was the beast's fault. It was mine. He was just doing what hairy beasts do—distracting me from healthy thoughts and tempting me to splatter my insecurities all over anyone within a 30-foot radius.

My earliest memory of feeling deeply affected by my hairy beast was the morning I arrived on a frost-covered playground, the first day back to school as a divorced kid. Two little girls stood under a big oak tree, oohing over what they got for Christmas. I broke in awkwardly to deliver my own holiday surprise.

"Oh no, I'm so sorry, Vanessa! You must be so sad!"

When I think back to that morning, I realize how compassionately those sweet girls behaved and how lucky I was to have had them as friends. But at the time, instead of feeling grateful for their concern, I felt angry at them. I felt offended that they dared to pretend to understand how I was feeling when their daddies would be home that night for pot roast and green beans. I was jealous, and I secretly hated them for having normal families. I wanted them to be damaged and worthless like I was, so I wouldn't feel so terribly alone. I didn't say that, of course.

"It's not a big deal. I'm not sad," I lied.

Without understanding my motivation, I spent my middle school years sabotaging unsuspecting peers. I gossiped and told unbecoming stories to make popular girls look bad. I made fun of pretty girls quietly to boys in hopes that those boys would find them unattractive. If anyone called me out, I'd manipulate my way out of it. I was not a good friend. I was not trustworthy. I was not kind.

I was not happy.

How could I be happy for those girls, with all their lightness and ease, while I was emotionally collapsing under the weight of a fractious and ugly hairy beast? The answer was, I couldn't. I didn't have the chops to rise above it all.

About half way through high school, I started to realize that tearing down powerful girls in a jealous rage was not an effective social strategy. Manipulating people was tiring and it only got me into trouble. My reindeer games sputtered to an end by tenth grade, thanks in part to a wholesome and collaborative group of girls I cheered with. As a pyramid base for the cheerleading team, I literally lifted girls up. I had a strong desire to keep them safe, to make them look good, to help my team by being a dependable foundation.

The physical experience of hoisting and catching girls' bodies seeped into my emotional experience of being a supportive girlfriend. Mind reflected body. My malevolent behavior faded unconsciously, like skin closing over a wound. Cheerleading assisted in healing a small but unruly part of my beastly anger, allowing a tiny, beautiful shift toward sister-friend love.

Three decades later, I've collected a thousand mean girl stories from women of all ages and backgrounds. In light of this friendly research, I'm confident in my belief that I'm not the only one who experienced trauma as a young girl, and that dramatic tween antics are here to stay. Early adolescent behavior is not a problem we need to solve; it's simply part of the human process.

Almost daily, my kids come home and report nasty things girls say and do to each other. They lie, they gossip, they push, they compete... sounds awfully familiar. I do not get bent out of shape when I hear about young girls back ending each other. I don't wish ill upon children or label them as bullies or bitches. Instead, I empower my own babies by teaching them to create durable energetic boundaries within themselves. I remind them that their friends may be dealing with tough stuff at home and urge them to be patient with kids who are deciding what kind of human they want to be. Adolescents need space to be assholes... and forgiveness when they realize they don't want to be assholes anymore. The less we condemn these mean girls, the sooner they'll figure it all out.

Healing

Anyone who knows me knows that I'm a girl's girl. I love women. I love to support women. I love to learn from women. I love to talk to women. I love being a woman. I am a collector of magnificent girlfriends and have many. (Perhaps I have too many, as I'm not able to see them all as much as I'd like.) My love for women was and is so great that the hairy-beast-inspired hurdle keeping me separate from the Sisterhood had to be the first to go, so divine grace shifted my mean girl status spontaneously, without my direction or effort.

Whether you want to call it divinity or maturity, we all have experiences of naturally rising out of our yuck, but there are times when we want to get unstuck from trauma-induced habits on purpose, consciously.

People often employ a combination of healing modalities like clinical therapy, prayer, exercise, or holistic wellness. Time, experience, and spontaneous revelation may be included in this list, too, along with a hundred other practices, like cheerleading. And then, of course, there is one that complements all of these modalities perfectly: mindfulness.

If you are like me and mindfulness is the foundational mental health practice you employ, you know that bringing fullness of presence into thoughts, speech, and actions provides useful insight into the sources of our topsoil triggers and allows us opportunity to acknowledge our struggle, experience it fully, then ease past it.

Within mindfulness, there is a diverse range of techniques, and I'll share plenty throughout this book. The most impactful for me has been writing meditation, which allows me to play Monday morning quarterback with traumatic experiences. Through this technique I have transmuted issues that I didn't even realize were getting in my way. I'll walk you through the process of meditative writing in chapter eight but wanted to share a sample now that demonstrates how I recently transmuted the karmic remains of my mean girl days.

Every time I scribble out this story, I find something new. Even from this vantage of middle age, there are nuggets of wisdom to uncover. The story is unchanged, but my maturity—or perhaps my mood—guides me to extract hidden insights that change me, and sometimes require peaceful action.

As I unearth memories today in my journal, an old feeling of shame rises. I close my eyes and scan for all the times I'd wronged a friend, all the times I'd hated someone for being admired, loved, or happy. My anger was not contained to middle school. There have been many moments since in which I'd acted out of jealousy or envied someone else's success.

I allow the more recent moments to rise with the old ones, invite them to break through the surface of this "now" moment as a cluster of suffering. The stories wrap around each other, thick and deeply rooted. Complicated feelings are attached. Shame, anger, isolation, confusion, and jealousy weigh heavy on my heart. My chest tightens. That tightness rises, squeezes at my throat, stings my eyes, and finally releases. Shame-filled teardrops spill over onto hot cheeks. Another feeling pushes up through the stories and into this moment. It, too, needs to be realized and reconciled: embarrassment. I allow that to rise and expose itself with the rest.

The feelings are strong; but I am stronger.

I write, sob, send silent love and apologies to those I've hurt. I close my eyes and visualize a tangled knot of feelings and stories in the ground by my feet.

I reach down and yank that shit up, roots and all.

I thank it for teaching me, then thank it for teaching everyone who will benefit from my story. I hold the root ball up high under the sun's eye and visualize it alchemizing into white light. When the root is gone, I take a deep breath in through the nose, so that my chest is completely saturated with oxygen. I hold my breath here at the top until it hurts, then release it slowly and loudly through my teeth. Sssssshhhhhhhhhhhhhhhh. I breathe in again. Sssssshhhhhhhhhhhhhhhh. One more time. Sssssshhhhhhhhhhhhhhhh.

I am not that girl anymore.

I AM.

Unstuck

I knew a goat once named Penelope. She lived on Sanctuary Farm in Sunapee, New Hampshire. She was small and white with horns about as long as the Dalai Lama's pointer finger. Penelope holds a special space in my heart because she and my daughter share a name… and because each time I saw her, she had her head stuck in a fence.

The goat would stand trapped, her eyes bored. Without struggle, she existed seemingly apathetically. It was as if she was patiently waiting for the pert tuft of grass below her chin to grow long enough to reach her mouth.

The first time I met Penelope, I sucked my teeth, sighed, reached for her. "Aww, poor thing," I gushed. My palms compassionately stroked her cone-shaped nose, hands gently pulled her horns forward and sideways, squeezing her head diagonally through thick wire and wood until she was free. A farmhand who stood nearby, watching, told me not to bother, said Penelope spends most of her days with her head stuck like that. I laughed in disbelief and judged him silently for not fixing the fence.

By the time I'd bought my corn and ice cream at the farm stand, Penelope's head was wedged in that hole again. The farmer shrugged and raised his eyebrows as if to say, *You can spring her again, but we both know what'll happen when you leave.*

I examined the goat and her surroundings. *This particular green grass tuft must taste better than the countless acres of perfectly accessible green grass tufts on her side of the fence*, I thought. Perhaps a visitor had dropped a tasty delight here once, and that sweet treat chronically haunted Penelope's one-track goat brain. Perhaps she yearned for a challenge that only this One Tuft of Grass offered.

Perhaps she'd lost her marbles.

Kneeling down, I whispered past her floppy ear, "I've been stuck, too, sister." Glancing sideways to make sure no one could see that I was life-coaching a goat, I confessed, "I had to remember that I deserve better, that I am worthy of freedom, that there's more to life than what I seem to be stuck with... and then everything changed for me."

She ignored me, stared vacantly, shifted her weight to settle in for a few more hours of green grass tuft growth. Maybe she wasn't ready to hear what I had to say. I sucked my teeth again, stood and walked away.

The only way to get unstuck and stay unstuck, is to unstick your damn self.

Don't I know it.

I've successfully stuck and unstuck myself from more situations than I care to count—from being a mean girl in junior high to a 22-year run of dysthymia, or low-grade depression. Even Michael and I got unstuck, amicably, after 13 years of marital reality. It took us several years to see we were unhappily, needlessly focused on one tuft of love that would never grow big enough to satisfy, and several more years to notice we each had the power to make a different choice. Our mutual liberation came only when we valued joy enough to risk the discomfort of changing our scenery. I share stories about my divorce throughout this book, but for a moment, let's talk about this idea of change.

Change

The thing that motherhood offers that differs from almost any other evolutionary path, is the unavoidable, constant, mandatory, in-our-face condition called change. We don't have to orchestrate change, it happens spontaneously and naturally, whether it's a chin whisker that sprouts on your son's otherwise hairless face or a stray kitten that follows your daughter home from school. These experiences breed potential and momentum—the exact conditions required for a rise out of the yuck.

Change is the opposite of being stuck.

Because you are a mother, you have an advantage. Unlike my

goat friend Penelope, you are an expert at forward movement, and that's just what you need to evolve. So, survey the creepy outskirts of your inner landscape. Scrutinize topsoil triggers that don't serve you. Allow yourself permission to poke at them and even weed them out. Your skillfully cultivated adaptability will cushion your body, mind, and spirit as you shake free of your hairy beast. And if you are ready to align with the energy of health and happiness, even at the expense of your immediate comfort, the Universe will organize around you to support your desires.

Chapter Summary:

May I get unstuck. May you get unstuck. May we get unstuck.

This chapter demonstrates an effective way to deal with your hairy beast through journaling. If your trauma involves something that's too painful to examine on your own, please practice this exercise under supervision of your therapist or doctor. Otherwise, start by acknowledging that journaling may be extremely uncomfortable and that you may hesitate or even dread getting started. The best way to get through your fear of discomfort is to approach the exercise with curiosity and neutrality. You are not your beast; your beast cannot hurt you anymore.

Journal Prompts:

- So, you met my hairy beast. What do you think of him? Is yours anything like mine?
- It seems that every time I hear someone tell a story of a powerful childhood event, it happens at age 11. Think back to the 11-year-old version of yourself. What happened? How does that experience inform your life today?
- Who are you today? Are you different than you were as a

kid? What remains? What have you grown into or out of?

- Is there some part of your life where you feel stuck? Is there anything holding you in this place? Are you sure?
- Is getting unstuck a priority for you? Why or why not?
- Recall the earliest bit of trauma you can remember. You may want to start by reflecting on the first time you shared your story out loud. Write down what you remember. Acknowledge two or three feelings that are attached to the story. Write them down, too. Search your mind for two or three times in your life that these feelings and stories have played into your relationships and behaviors. Keep writing. When you're done digging, sit back and examine it all. Take your time. Pull out the lesson, thank the bullshit, and turn it all to light.

3

May I remember. May you remember. May we remember.

Bra

In seventh grade, I was the shortest kid in my class and so skinny, gangly, and flat-chested I looked like a walking skeleton. At age 12, I was the only girl in school who didn't wear a bra. One adolescence defining afternoon in the cafeteria, a pale-faced, wide-mouthed boy locked his eyes on my chest from the head of the lunch table and bleated: "BRRRAAAAA! BRRRAAAAA! BRRRAAAAA!" Imagine a pubescent sheep at full volume and you've got the tenor of his delivery.

His relentless performance endured for about 40 seconds. The boy was rewarded with group laughter so intense, tears came more readily than sound. My response was to pretend it wasn't happening. I dropped my head and stared into my Oscar Mayer sandwich, equal parts horrified and humiliated. Surely, they'd forgotten I was human. I changed tables the next day and avoided eye contact with that kid for three years.

Lying in bed that night, I recalled a moment in the lunchroom from the day before, when one of my girlfriends snuck up behind me while I was tossing my brown paper lunch bag in the trash. She pulled at the back of my turtleneck sweater, as if to snap a bra strap.

"Oops!" she mused. "You don't wear one."

The next day sheep boy gave his grand performance. Putting

two and two together, I realized there had likely been considerable lunch table speculation on my state of puberty, spearheaded by someone I had believed to be a friend.

It hurt. I cried.

Since it seemed that half the school wanted me to wear a bra, I mustered the nerve to ask my mother for a shopping trip to the lingerie department at Jordan Marsh. The next year, eighth grade, I was a newly minted 13-year-old, sitting in the cafeteria with my girlfriends, chatting and goofing. I was wearing a white t-shirt, just sheer enough to show the outline of my ingloriously procured bra. When I felt a tap on my shoulder, I turned around to see a kind boy with whom I'd always been friendly. "Vanessa," he said. His face was bright red. I thought maybe he wanted to ask me out. Everyone was staring at us. "I can't do it. I can't do it." He shuffled back to his table, head down, all his friends keeling over, whooping loudly, holding their bellies.

I returned to my lunch and a few minutes later, the boy tapped my shoulder again. Same thing. His, "I can't do it," was followed by another round of knee slapping and crowing from the boys' table across the cafeteria. A few more minutes passed; I felt another tap. I spun around this time to see a different boy—a friend of the first and, I had thought, a friend of mine. "Vanessa!" he hollered. "WHY DO YOU WEAR A BRA???!!!!"

The lunchroom ripped open.

High fives. Red faces. Hysteria.

Boys were laughing so hard they were falling off their seats. All I could do was sit there with my jaw dropped, living a teenage nightmare. I felt exposed and deeply ashamed, targeted and humiliated. Rejection comes in all shapes and sizes, and that afternoon it came in size 32-AAA.

I have fuzzy memories of history teachers, algebra classes, and school dances in junior high. Lunch hour is crystal clear.

Memories

Several years later, while seeking parenting advice in a book called *The Whole-Brain Child* by Dan Siegel and Tina Payne Bryson, I was surprised to extract break-through insight into my own childhood.

They described *implicit memories* as things that we learn and are recalled unconsciously, automatically. When we type on a keyboard or ride a bike, we don't think about the moments we first learned how—we just do it. For better or for worse, experiences can automate emotions in the same way. Every time we encounter something that has faint resemblance to emotional trauma that we've programmed implicitly, our brain unconsciously categorizes the new experience accordingly and generates the emotions that correspond. In my case, no one had to remind me that I was ugly and wretched, I'd learned it through traumatic interactions with my peers and implicitly carried that misguided truth forward into other parts of my life.

For those haunted by public humiliation like me, our wonder years may have looked something like this: not invited to a birthday party? *Bam! I am an outcast.* Dumped by a boyfriend? *Flash! I am discardable.* Not voted to Student Council? *Crack! I am unworthy.* Unfortunately, maturity doesn't heal our implicit memories. Just like acne and mood swings, these hairy little beasts chase us into adulthood: turned down for your dream job? *Kapow! I am not good enough!* Your kid tanks his basketball team tryout? *Boom! He's a loser just like his mom.* These implicits silently connect the dots between past and present experiences without us knowing they're doing it.

There's a saying in science, coined by neuropsychologist Donald Hebb back in 1949, "Neurons that fire together wire together." Each time a perceived stress occurs, the neural pathways connecting the stress, emotions, and sensations get stronger and stronger; through this well-worn connection, we learn to react to stressful situations by feeling (fill in the blank). For me, the blank was filled by humiliation, rejection, inadequacy, and shame. Those feelings became my standard social knee-jerk.

The most distinctly painful memories I hold from adolescence revolve around being rejected and left out. I fell to pieces if I wasn't invited to a sleepover or a Friday night trip to Westgate Mall. As an adult recalling this, I think, *That's crazy! I had lots of friends and got invited to tons of outings.* But as a kid in the yuck, I couldn't see straight, couldn't hear the nice things people said to me. The majority of my experiences took the familiar neural railway straight to Loserville.

I unconsciously filtered many years of experiences through implicit memories, assigning meaning and purpose, to protect myself from tangles with hairy beasts. But I assigned the wrong meaning and the wrong purpose and continued to do so until I dragged those unconscious little implicits, wailing and moaning to the surface of awareness, where I could integrate them with explicit memories, or conscious memories.

Explicit memories are consciously formed memories—specific personal events that we recall with ease. When implicit becomes explicit, our automatic responses to potential stress take on clearer meaning, and we can actually make sense of it all. As we learn to respond insightfully to stimuli, like rejection, we forge new neural pathways in the brain, creating limitless, and perhaps beneficial, possibilities and outcomes.

With mindfulness practice, emotions and their sources remain exposed in the light where they can be seen clearly. No more hairy beasts lurking in dark corners, waiting to jump out and wrestle us to the topsoil when we feel vulnerable or stressed. But if we cannot become conscious of implicit memories, we are doomed to pass them on to our kids.

Seriously, this shit does not disappear on its own, my friend. The sooner we deal with implicits, the sooner we stop dumping our karma on our babies.

Lunch

When my daughters started elementary school, I found myself very protective over their experiences in the cafeteria. I'd question them daily about the way they were being treated by peers during lunch. Their lunch period became my topsoil trigger.

I didn't make the connection until I started writing this book. Recreating that lunchroom scene in vivid detail forced my implicit feelings to the surface where I could examine them and see how they affected my present-day interactions. Now, I am mindful of my tendency to grill the kids about lunch antics and check myself: *This is MY issue, not theirs*. I engage my freedom to choose another neural path. I zip my lips, take a breath, and let my babies teach me that the cafeteria can be a fun, safe place to enjoy good friends. No more hand-me-down yuck.

This is just one of many times I've used mindfulness and writing to rewire habitual categorization of experiences. The heaviest piece of implicit rejection—the piece that involved my father abandoning me—was a little more complicated to clear.

Awesomeness

At age 11, the concept of abandonment was introduced, and my mind instinctively generated an intimate, first-hand definition of rejection. Rejection, and the physiological reactions that accompanied it, became an implicit memory—a silent current that has rocked the undercarriage of my experiences from the day my father rolled out of the driveway in his olive-green Jetta.

When I was about 33, I wrote down my abandoned little girl story, conjuring pre-adolescence, dredging details, reliving emotion, the whole bit. This took a long time, months and months. When it was all recorded, I read that story aloud until I could do it without crying. I didn't realize it at the time, but this practice kept my deeply rooted emotional wounds exposed so they could be clearly seen and consciously healed.

While all that yuck was exposed, I engaged a superhero-style mindfulness tool that I learned in a book called *Making a Change for Good* by Zen master Cheri Huber. I started wearing my watch on the wrong wrist so that the discomfort would remind me to notice my thoughts. It was sort of like tying a ribbon around my finger, but less conspicuous. Every time I'd think something reject-y like, *My neighbor is having a party and didn't invite me because I'm a loser*, the uncomfortable watch would trigger my awareness and I'd correct the thought, *Nope. That's not true. Because I'm not 11, and I'm actually kind of awesome.* It was a little Jack Handy, but so what? It worked. (Look for more ideas like the watch trick in chapter five.)

This transformation toward awesomeness can take place over hours or years. It all depends on your readiness to heal and your willingness to take action.

It sounds so simple, because it can be simple if you let it be. **Your responses to stress and trauma are in your complete control.** You just have to: one, believe it; and two, allow it.

Chapter Summary:

May I remember. May you remember. May we remember.

Implicit memories get filed deep in your subconscious mind, where you create knee-jerk emotional assessments that turn into misguided personal truth. This truth may not be real Truth, but you believe it is, and this belief is the foundation for your future. When implicit becomes explicit, you heal old emotional wounds and your misguided truth comes into question.

Journal Prompts:
- Is deep healing something you are ready for right now? ("No" is an acceptable answer.) What efforts have you made to heal? What worked? Why? What didn't? Why not?
- I pushed my brood on lunchroom behavior. What is the one thing you push your kids on the hardest? What was your experience of this activity as a child? Don't flit around on the surface of this question. Get really honest with yourself, even if you feel uncomfortable.
- Name one gnarly thing you believe to be implicitly true about yourself. Where and when did that story originate?
- Implicit memories are not always bad. Call out some of your implicit awesomeness. How does this filter through to your babies?
- What is your capital-T-Truth? If you don't know yet, leave this blank and come back to it regularly.

4

May I be healthy. May you be healthy. May we be healthy.

Poop

My sophomore year at Bentley, a prestigious New England business college, was pretty uncomfortable. My father made a flash appearance in my life after six years of radio silence. He wrote me a creepy letter about the two of us dying together, accompanied by a check for $35—an underwhelming attempt to make up for 84 months of missed child support payments and a whopping $0.00 contribution to my college education. He then showed up to a football game where I was cheerleading, at which point I tossed my blue and gold pom-poms on the track and fled home to my dorm where I cowered under blankets with a bottle of Absolut Citron.

I had never reconciled my feelings about being abandoned by my father and this strange, brief cameo really fucked me up. I started smoking a lot of weed and sleeping through early morning classes. My grades plummeted. I lost my scholarships and financial aid and had to transfer to a small state school.

For years after this failure spiral, I suffered from daily bouts of diarrhea and excruciating belly pains. At the time, I was convinced I had Crohn's Disease, but my doctor couldn't prove it. She never asked me about my mental health, never probed into my life story. Based on my symptoms, she guessed I had IBS, Irritable Bowel Syndrome, paired with lactose intolerance. She told me to stop eating greasy food and drinking milk, prescribed Imodium AD, and sent me on my way.

Armed with a three-month supply of Lactaid pills and a handbag stuffed with soft toilet paper, I repeated second-semester freshman year at Bridgewater State studying broadcast journalism. I could barely make the commute to campus without cramping up. I would park my car and haul ass to the closest bathroom. By junior year, I had reached the point of no longer waiting until the ladies' room was empty before getting sick. There was just no time anymore. Pretty girls applied lip gloss at the mirror as I'd sprint into a stall four feet away, purging my innards and gasping for air as if I'd just been chased by a lion.

Once I had to miss a class because I was stuck in the loo. I told my professor the truth about why I wasn't in class. A stickler for attendance, however, he was apathetic and unyielding. Despite my begging and near perfect scores, he docked me severely on my final grade for the one unexcused absence, causing me to miss magna cum laude by a fraction of a tenth of a percent. (That guy was an asshole.)

Missing class was only the beginning of the missing out I'd experience during my co-ed years. I visited The Louvre in Paris as a 20-year-old backpacker. As I turned the corner to see the *Mona Lisa,* a wave of tummy panic shot through me. Crushed, I groaned to my travel companions that I wasn't going to make it to Lisa's bulletproof glass case, then sprinted down two floors to the toilets, only to find a line 30 tourists deep. The next hour was a blur—a series of jerky Metro cars and filthy standing toilets between the Louvre and my Latin Quarter hostel—a *trés unique* self-guided Parisian tour. To this day, every time I see the *Mona Lisa*, I die a little inside.

Distance

During my senior year, The Washington Center awarded me an internship with Tribune Broadcasting, the *Chicago Tribune*'s broadcast news shop. I moved to Washington D.C. in January of 1998 to work at their national bureau. This was a small agency that relied heavily on its two full-time interns for field production, and I worried about my IBS holding me back.

For my first big assignment, my boss sent me to former President Bill Clinton's State of the Union address. The job was to scan the jam-packed Capitol Rotunda for congressional representatives from our 19 affiliate territories, guide them to the *Tribune*'s interview station, and chat them up while they awaited their turn to talk to our reporter. That night, there was no space for insecurity, no time to be sick. This would prove to be the case for the months to follow.

With the Lewinsky scandal in full force, I spent many weeks in The White House Press Room logging soundbites from Press Secretary Mike McCurry. Occasionally Mike would call us in for a *gaggle briefing,* an info session that took place in his private office, off-camera but on-record. Talk about no space for sickness... I'd stand wedged shoulder to shoulder in this tiny office between Sam Donaldson, Helen Thompson, and a dozen other White House correspondents, feverishly scribbling notes to bring back to base, hoping I could provide something juicy for the on-air report that night.

My daily assignments thrilled and challenged me. This exciting, power-packed world required that I deliver the very best of myself. With nobody from home around to remind me I was a ridiculous, disposable loser, I easily reinvented, rising to meet the needs of my job. IBS symptoms disappeared for the entire five months I lived in the Beltway.

Psst

There's a saying, "If you listen when your body whispers, you won't have to hear it scream." Though my respite from IBS was temporary, I did hear a tiny whisper: *Psst, Vanessa. Did you notice you felt healthy when you moved away? This pooping issue may not be about your love of ice cream. Maybe you should look at what's happening at home.*

Our bodies speak to us all the time. Most people don't listen. For all sorts of reasons, we power through belly pains, rashes, and ringing ears in hopes that eventually physical discomforts will go away on their own. Even if we do behave responsibly and see a doctor, often times our problems are beyond obvious medical explanation, so we go home and continue to suffer. **Sister, you know this as well as I do: our minds and bodies reflect each other constantly. Heal one, and the other falls in line.** Connecting any and all dots between the two lead to deliberate, healthy changes.

Mind-body techniques can help us understand why we're suffering and manage stress related physical symptoms and chronic pain resulting from illnesses such as IBS, arthritis, fibromyalgia, autoimmune disease, anxiety, etc. The following are three techniques I used to help me dig down to the root of my own health issue.

Conscious consumption. Eating mindfully can help us to distinguish which foods are unsettling to our bellies while we're eating them. Present-moment awareness saves us from future discomfort. Heighten your awareness of the food you eat. This means slowing down while eating and paying attention to the way the body reacts as food enters it. Keep a food journal—write down everything you ingest, recalling your mindful observations, and recording your poops in detail. (Draw pictures. It's so funny.) Dairy is an obvious stimulant for many people suffering from IBS, but there are others: gluten, sweets, and even meat. An elimination diet is ideal for figuring out what works for your body. Need more help with this one? Dr. Judson Brewer of the University of Massachusetts Center for Mindfulness developed an app called *Eat Right Now* that teaches students how to gain control over eating habits through a series of short videos. (Suffering from allergies? This can help with that as well.)

Distance. Hold this book an inch from your face. Try to get a good look at your surroundings. Now, still holding the book, extend your arms all the way out. By creating some distance between your face and the book, you are able to see the bigger picture. The book is still there, but it doesn't consume your perspective. Pain affects your outlook in the same way. Extreme discomfort gets right in your face and may cause you to panic. **Panic is just a temporary loss of perspective.** Changing your environment or routine creates physical distance between you and your suffering, allowing a shift in perspective that relaxes panicky thoughts, as well as provides opportunity for healing. If physical distance is not possible, you can also create emotional distance through meditation. We'll explore this in chapter nine.

Reinvention. Remember that you have a superhero advantage: the ability to accept change and thrive in it. Sometimes, when you're feeling physically ill, there's nothing wrong with you. You're just stuck. Getting unstuck will unstick the illness. In chapter 10, we'll talk about ways to release habits, situations, and relationships that no longer serve you; reflect in the empty space you've created after the release; and redirect your focus toward wholesome habits, situations, and relationships.

Management

While digging for long-term solutions, it's important to attempt short-term relief. I'd love to tell you that the following techniques obliterate pain, but in my experience, they really just help me manage it.

Breath. Focusing on breath may help you while in the throes of a belly busting episode. Breathe in through the nose, deep and strong, for a count of seven. Then release the breath out through an O-shaped mouth, long and slow and controlled, for a count of 11. Let the chest rise and fall for the first few breaths then try to spread the breath into your fingertips. Relax the hands, breathe out. Remind yourself that this is just a moment. It won't last forever. Use the next painful twist to release whatever is inside of you.

Distraction. Sometimes when you're in immense physical discomfort, the last thing you want to do is think about your body or the breath that's moving through it. But there are always parts of your body that don't hurt, like your left big toe or the tip of your nose. So, if you find yourself doubled over on the toilet wanting to tear out of your skin, pour all of your brainpower into a neutral body part. Get curious about it. Let it distract you from the stabbing in your gut—even if for a moment.[3] Distraction can calm the body, settle the shakes, quell the sweats, distract the fear, and normalize the airflow.

Meditation. Sit alone in a safe place when your belly is feeling neutral, set your intention specifically on healing your IBS (*feel* the *feeling* of being completely healed, and if you can hold onto that feeling for a good 90 seconds, all the better), and then release your

---

[3]You could perhaps use a mantra as a distraction as well, but I find that it's hard to get the volume of your mantra to override the physical discomfort. We'll learn more about mantras in chapter nine.

intention. Just focus on the breath. Thoughts and doubts and boredom will pop into your mind. Just say hello to them all and return focus to your breath. You may have to sit a few times with this intention, maybe over a week or two. But when you have a problem that gets in your way like IBS does, progress should not take long. Higher thinking, which is a side effect of meditation, points you toward clear solutions.

Ships

After I completed the internship and returned home to Massachusetts, my tummy woes resurfaced. Throughout my final semester at Bridgewater State and well beyond college graduation, my anxiety over IBS caused me to stop doing any activity without a guaranteed restroom. The times I did venture into *Unknown Pottyland*, I'd limit myself to a diet of bagels, green apples, and Imodium AD. I became so dependent on Imodium that I ended up in the emergency room twice, bound with loperamide-induced cramps that were eventually rivaled only by labor pains.[4] Adventure wasn't worth the risk. Riding the T, going to the beach, jogging, hiking, biking, golfing, road-tripping… all nixed. Work, bars, home, the gym, and my good-hearted-but-stuck-in-his-own-way boyfriend's apartment were safe havens. For the most part, these were not lively places. I became dull, depressed.

My sister saw I was unwell and offered help. She had spent five years working as entertainment staff onboard a luxury cruise ship line and convinced me that sailing would drown my blues.

She was right.

In the fall of 1999, I boarded the *MS Maasdam* as entertainment

---

[4] I had my three from-scratch babies vaginally, without epidural, and if on a scale of 1-10 the "ring of fire" that burns the cervix just before it's time to push is a 10, these cramps were an 8.5.

staff; my years of desperately seeking sanitation faded into the past. The ship was a perfect place for me because there were toilets absolutely everywhere—clean ones with flushing power that would thrill George Costanza.

I never had to worry.

Moreover, much like my college internship, the *Maasdam* was completely devoid of my past—a sturdy, safe vessel built for escape and reinvention. Because I was traveling and mobile phones were rare, no one at home expected me to check in, so I completely checked out of my life. I played games with passengers all day, visited ports from Nicaragua to Norway, made amazing new friends, ate delicious food, exercised regularly in the sunshine, and found a relaxed new version of myself amidst happy adventures. I felt free and safe for the first time in years. The distance I created between myself and my problems allowed me opportunity to get composed and see the bigger picture. The IBS healed, and I began to consciously wonder if the condition was in my head—less about physical illness, more about mental illness. That didn't mean my IBS wasn't real; it just meant that if I could mentally keep my shit together (haha), I'd be okay.

Graduate

Eventually, I had to go home and figure out a way to feel healthy on land. In 2001, I moved back to Massachusetts and lived with my mom and stepdad George. They were a stable and loving team who supported me while, at age 25, I finally started making some careful, healthy decisions. The first was disconnecting from toxic people: a couple of close friends and a longtime boyfriend.

The slate already felt cleaner.

I found a fun job, moved to Boston, saved money, partied a little less, and finally connected with a seasoned psychotherapist.

My therapist Linda and I got right to work on my daddy issues and spent a year exploring the way Pop's rejection had decimated my self-worth. Simply put, when I got close to any experience that felt joyful, exciting, or rewarding, my subconscious would be like, *Nope. You don't deserve that. You're not worthy of feeling carefree. You don't get to be loved or have fun. Vanessa, you need to stay where you belong: dull and depressed. Cue the tummy; it's time to poop.*

We used a technique called EMDR (Eye Movement Desensitization and Reprocessing) to process the initial trauma of abandonment. As I released old miscreated truths, I learned new ways to see my adult self, not as a victim or as a child or as someone who deserves a crappy life, but as a beautiful, empowered young woman who just might be worthy of good things. I finally graduated from the School of IBS. It's not something I put on my resume, but it might be the best degree I've ever earned.

Tarzan

Those years of IBS were a strange sort of trauma for me. Even after the symptoms cleared, I habitually continued to behave as if I were sick, not straying far from bathrooms and often seeking safer, more sedentary activities.

This remained the case for a couple of years, which became a problem when I met Michael's family, a tribe of hardcore hikers. Holidays and vacations were always punctuated with an aggressive tromp up a nearby mountaintop. Not wanting to be left behind, I would tuck a roll of Charmin in my backpack and join the crowd. Inevitably, I'd notice my belly squeezing—typically as we entered the trailhead—and remind myself the sensation was just an old habit dying hard. I could almost always breathe deeply to get through it.

One summer day, while hiking in Maine, the family was thrilled to find a stunning natural pool surrounded by stone waterslides. High on a rocky ledge, a tattered rope beckoned the group. By this time, I was a new mother. I held baby Penelope and watched from the safety of the river bank as my nieces and nephews bounded up the ledge, grabbed hold of the rope, and rode that sucker with delight into the water.

While I was slowly acclimating to exploring the world again—not the dreamy cruise ship world but *my real-life* world—the uninhibited adventurer in me had long been dormant. I was surprised to hear an inner voice whisper, *Live it up, V. Jump!* After avoiding *real-life* happiness for so many years, I never considered that rope could be for me. But the words buzzed my ears again: *Live your life, Vanessa.*

I heard the whisper this time.

No screaming necessary.

I blinked twice then handed Penelope to a nearby niece. I scrambled up the cliff and somehow mustered to the courage to grab hold of that splintered rope and Tarzan my way to a breathtaking moment. It was like being born again. I'd missed out on so much because I was mentally chained to the safety of a bathroom. I had forgotten how fun it was to be alive and spontaneous... how deserving I was of fun.

I was 29 when I grabbed that rope. Man, did it take me a long time to start living. Many years later, while journaling, I connected all the dots between those experiences and more. Abandonment led to self-hatred to depression to self-sabotage to IBS... which led to anxiety and more limitation and more depression. Sometimes the depression led to lethargy, back pain, headaches, and mood swings. Other times the dots connected to thoughts of suicide. There were many hard years leading up to the point when my experience of depression finally began to decongest at age 33, but here's the thing about depression I'm undyingly grateful for: **When you're really deep in the hole, you can't help but think about the light.** It's way down in that hole you can get humble enough to start looking for God. You're so damn desperate for a miracle that you drop your filter; you start wanting to see fairies and ghosts and statues that cry. You're like, *If that bush in my front yard bursts into flames, I won't kill myself today. Come on bush. Light up. You can do it. Wait. Was that a spark? Nah. Just a candy wrapper caught in its branches. But it sorta-kinda looked like a spark, so I'll put death off for one more day.*

Martin Luther King said it best: "Only in the darkness can you see the stars."

Chapter Summary:
   May I be healthy. May you be healthy. May we be healthy.

Knowing that the mind and body are connected is a fundamental step toward healing. I wonder if I would have spared myself pain and suffering, had I been introduced to an insight practice as an adolescent. Back then I would have done anything to be normal, to feel good. But today, I'm grateful for all those yuck-filled experiences. The yuck humanized me in a way "normal" never could have.

Journal Prompts:
- Do you deserve good health?
- Are you worthy of healthy relationships with people, food, and environment?
- The mind and body nest together, mirror each other. What does your body say to you every day? What does your mind say back?

- What suffering do you accommodate that keeps you unhealthy? Are you interested in relieving yourself of the suffering? If not, why? If yes, why now? Why not before? What's changed?

5

May I feel like sunshine. May you feel like sunshine. May we feel like sunshine.

Bold

One of the points I drive home throughout *Metta Mom* is that your emotional challenges won't disappear on their own. **You are far too accommodating to your internal suffering.** If you're stuck—be it in a feeling or a relationship or a habit—you are the only one who can unstick yourself. That may mean bootstrapping your way out of your yuck like I did, or it may mean seeking therapy of some sort. Whatever you choose, it starts with you deciding that you deserve happiness and continues with you taking action that helps you heal.

Some of my stories represent big picture healing. They tell about situations where I take bold action to break apart big, chunky pieces of depression. The subtle healing, the more nuance-y, revelatory stuff where hidden issues are brought to light and transmuted, is all done through mindful awareness. These tiny shifts happen quietly and unexpectedly, but because my awareness is heightened, I am able to pick up on insights and apply them to my healing process. This is why inviting mindfulness into your healing efforts helps you unstick faster and dissolve chunky pieces of your suffering more completely.

Healing is a forever practice. Life constantly presents you with new challenges, new temptations, and new relationships to learn from. Remembering that you deserve happiness prevents you from getting buried in needless drama; and when you bump into drama that you do need, you must work your healing tools confidently and without hesitation.

Rain

During humbling times, I've engaged some low-vibrational behaviors: mood swings, crabbiness, insomnia or nightmares, forgetfulness, despondence, jealousy, lack of productivity, and a hundred more undesirable qualities. Because I'm determined to raise my vibe, I've had to find ways to acknowledge my experience of depression without blowing up my life or making people cringe when I enter a room. Awareness of depressive stimulants can help you to prepare for challenges and perhaps cut them off early. An easy stimulant to identify is change of season.

Seasonal transitions can be overwhelming; these are times we may feel shocked by shifts in temperature, sunlight, routines, holidays, and even sports seasons. Maybe it's the springtime pressure to sign the kids up for activities that they won't beg to quit after two days… or slogging through the mall for back-to-school clothes with one girl who hates everything and one girl who wants everything… or perhaps it's the mixed-emotions of summer vacation. Once upon a time, the last day of school was a magical door that led to a world twirling with possibilities. Now, it feels a little more like no-man's land: either we spend magical days with kids and compromise work hours, or we spend a bloody fortune on camps and sitters, hungrily waiting for dinner time when we gobble up their stories of fun and sun.

Maybe it's purely weather-related. One particular week two years ago, Mother Nature provided umpteen straight days of raw spring rain in New England. My lawn looked like an Irish postcard;

47

my mind looked like the underground Demogorgon lair in *Stranger Things*. I became sluggish, directionless, unmotivated. These qualities, while undesirable for professional production, were perfect for napping. So rather than fight my biology, I surrendered to it. I came into my office on a particularly drizzly morning, made a nest of meditation cushions and blankets on the floor, and took a snooze. I felt cozy and protected. The rain outside lulled me to sleep and I woke up feeling supported and restored. I actually walked down the hall after, bragging to officemates, "Hey y'all! Guess what I just did?" Weather-induced mood crisis averted.

Napping isn't the only way to manage heavy weather days. Later that same year during a summer scorcher, the kids and I were sandal shopping downtown when a wild rainstorm blew in. Main Street flooded within five minutes. I looked at my bored, barefoot kids and spontaneously yelped, "Everyone out the door for puddle jumping!" They squealed and bolted outside. Within seconds we were soaked from tip to toe, laughing hysterically. I took a picture of Penelope reveling in this storm, mouth wide open, head thrown back with joy, and later framed it. It was one of the best afternoons of my motherhood.

Winter

The most challenging seasonal transition, by far, is the onset of winter. The encroachment of sunlight-starved days turns me into a dead woman walking. Early December feels like Susan Sarandon squeezing my shoulder from behind, whispering Isaiah 43:1. Since a reunion with the almighty is a rather impractical way to manage the winter blues, below is a list of mindful doables I've practiced successfully so that I can be the sun when I can't see the sun.

Plan short-term projects. Write 10 poems, organize your closet, volunteer for the day at an animal shelter, host a potluck brunch.

Exercise. Get yourself to the gym or out for a brisk walk at least once a week. Partner up with a friend who will keep you accountable. (Or, if you can afford it, sign on with a personal trainer and ask them to hold you to weekly sessions.)

Meditate. Experiment with new techniques, listen to different body scans on YouTube, try chakra meditations at local yoga studios.

Wash your hands. Nothing spells "Pit of Despair" like influenza.

Journal. You can't be grateful and sad at the same time, so log 10 things you're thankful for once a day.

RSVP. Missing social events because you're feeling depressed sucks; but feeling guilty about bagging is even worse. Give yourself permission to RSVP "no" to invitations but push yourself to commit to one outing each month with people you truly like—even if that means lassoing a friend or two for a monthly trip to the movies— and be sure to show up mentally and physically.

Shine. Indulge in some good old-fashioned retail therapy (do not buy anything black); or find inexpensive, creative ways to incorporate bright color into your look (fingernails, undies, necklaces, gloves, socks, etc.). Multi-colored toenails are my go-to.

Recharge. Buying *things* is only a temporary pick-me-up—we know this. Purchasing an experience has long-term benefits. Not only does it give you something to look forward to, but it also colors your conversations, potentially for years after.

Spark a light. There's something about a glowing candle that makes you feel alive and peaceful. Pick up some natural, mildly scented candles. Lavender is good for relaxation and lemon will invigorate you.

Discuss. Don't suffer in a vacuum. Tell a friend what you're experiencing and ask for help on bad days. Honestly, you don't even have to force chit-chat. I used to call my BFF, Lynne, and we would just breathe on the phone with each other while we watched trashy reality shows. We'd talk on commercial breaks.

And speaking of vacuums. Vacuum. An old roommate once told me, "If you're ever feeling depressed, clean your room. It makes you feel so much better." He was right.

Serve others. Shovel snow for a neighbor, cook a big stew and deliver it to a sick friend, do something that broadens your perspective and produces positive results. Sometimes when we're depressed, we lose our sense of purpose. We forget there's a big world outside our door that needs us. Be brave, reach out, and work hard.

Eat well. It's so easy to ravage a pan of brownies when you're depressed or to go the other way and starve yourself (due to feeling turned off by food or the effort it takes to prepare it). Modify expectations and commit to one healthy meal per day or even just one serving of whole food, like an apple.

Drink water. Fatigue, hunger, sluggishness, bad mood, headache, and nausea can all be symptoms of one thing: dehydration. When I don't feel right and can't figure out what's wrong, I usually feel better after a glass of water.

Lay off the booze. Numbing the pain won't erase it. Alcohol, a depressant, may worsen your situation by causing you to do dumb things, feel sick, or get puffy. If sobriety turns you off, it might be time to talk to someone about addiction.

Unplug. Log out of Facebook and Instagram. Seeing families on fun vacations and watching cat videos is not good when you're feeling stuck. The amount of free time you gain after logging out will surprise you, so consciously plan a way to fill that space with something productive, maybe with something else on this list. (See chapter 13 for help on this.)

Hike. Winter hikes in the snow are amazing. Bring friends, pets, or children. Getting into nature and enjoying the sunshine are the best seasonal depression defenses.

Medicate. If you are in a bad place and cannot find a way out, talk to your doctor. Not everyone can manage depression on their own. There is no shame in taking medication to get over the hump. Just be sure to ask about an exit strategy as you accept a prescription.

Fruit

Except for the medication, I've done all these things during bouts of depression—seasonal, transitional, or otherwise—but probably my favorite blues-buster is handing out fresh fruit to homeless folks.

Next time you go into the city, bring a big bag of oranges and bananas to distribute. Imagine the burst of flavor in a hungry person's mouth as he bites into a juicy orange. Bananas are sweet and delicious and, as an added bonus, look like happy smiles.

You don't have to wait until the depths of February to try this activity out. During a summer heat wave a few years back, Xavier and I packed a rolling suitcase with fruit, bottled water, and protein bars then hopped a train to Boston Common where we delivered snacks for two hours. We rode home, sweaty and tired, but overall feeling pretty darn good. As we rumbled up the track, I asked Xavier what he learned that day. He considered, then said, "Next time we do this we shouldn't bring apples because most of the people didn't have teeth."

Two things struck me in his observation: one, his pragmatism; and two, his promise of a "next time." There are a lot of ways we could have spent two hours on a scorching summer day, and this outing met his approval.

I felt hopeful.

Hope leaves little room for depression.

Chapter Summary

May I feel like sunshine. May you feel like sunshine. May we feel like sunshine.

After experiencing depression once, mental health professionals say that you are more vulnerable to experiencing depression again. A revisit with the blues can result from topsoil triggers, new trauma, illness or injury, sudden change, or just because.

These experiences are neutral, but most of the time your feelings about them are anything but. It is possible to shine like the sun, even in the worst of conditions, if you respond to experiences with action and mindful awareness, trusting that you really do deserve happiness.

Journal Prompts:

- Are you ever upset by changes of season? How about your kids? Do they act funny when the weather changes? Add to the list of things you can do during seasonal transitions to help you cope.
- What other types of transitions are hard for you and your babies? Vacations? Back to school? New friends? A death of a loved one or pet? What do you do to help them that works? Do you ever feel short tempered or impatient?
- Which season is your favorite? Name something you look forward to in each season. How can you amplify those things you most look forward to? Can you involve your children in some of those blues-busting activities?

6

May I love my period. May you love your period. May we love our period.

Flow

Let's hang here in the land of moodiness and suffering for just a bit longer and talk menses—specifically PMS.[5]

I have a love/hate relationship with my period. I love it because my uterus is downright miraculous, and menstruation is its required maintenance. I hate it because tampons give me a headache, and PMS gives me a bad attitude.

Aunt Flow consumes at least half of our reproductive years. That's an extraordinary amount of time to share headspace with an invisible force who makes a very believable case that we are all actually lunatics.

Have you ever read *The Red Tent* by Anita Diamant? It's the story of the Old Testament's Jacob and his multitude of wives. The red tent is an annex filled with hay beds where biblical village women would spend each full moon cycle. Our female ancestors menstruated simultaneously and would leave their men and boys in the competent hands of young girls who hadn't yet started monthly

---

[5] Two of many reasons I considered taking this section out of *Metta Mom*: Not every woman experiences PMS, and not every woman can mind-body her way to relief. But in the end, I decided it would be irresponsible to write a book about mothering without talking about monthlies.

bleeding and old women who'd survived the transition out of the cycle. So basically, once a month, young women enjoyed a whole week spinning stories and teaching each other life skills in a cozy tent without the pressure of men demanding blowjobs or seconds of mutton stew. Honestly, I think it sounds kind of awesome. I'm seriously considering erecting a red tent in my backyard.

The only reason I hesitate to bunk with a bunch of menstruating 21st century women is that we can be truly awful creatures when Aunt Flow moves in. She arrives in our bodies up to a week early with her crappy attitude, her heavy suitcases, and her complaints about our cooking. She sweats and thrashes in our bed and micromanages our relationships. She stains our Hanky Pankies and gives us the runs. She yells at our kids and pigs out on their Halloween candy while they're at school. Half our adult life (two weeks of every month!), we share a dwelling with this home-wrecker and force our friends and families to operate under her grueling regime.

What do you say, mommies? Let's take control and build a little red tent out back—just for Flow—create some space between her and us. Then we can move about our homes in peace and maybe even teach our daughters how to manage their menses with greater ease. Sounds fab, right? How do we do this?

We women are generally so out of touch with natural body rhythms that when our crazy sets in we can't see that it's hormonal hocus-pocus. We might pick fights with friends, feel offended by co-workers, or convince ourselves that our children are purposely not flushing the toilet to spite us. We weep, we gorge on potato chips, we terrorize our significant other, and we press the snooze button over and over, all the while believing wholeheartedly that this is who we are. But here's the newsflash, sisters: Our anger and our cravings are not real.

There's an old saying, "When you hear the beating of hooves, look for horses, not zebras." **When we are suffering with PMS, rather than spiraling into self-condemnation for lashing out at anyone remotely annoying, remember the period is to blame, not some major personality flaw.** (There's a cotton pony joke in here, but I'll show restraint.)

Welcome to the fast track to enlightenment via the feminine aisle:

Use a calendar to keep track of your period. Observe your behavior in the 7-10 days before you bleed. Each time you are short with your co-worker or critical of your mother-in-law, each time you feel insecure about a friendship or explosively frustrated with your kids, each time you gorge on baked goods or sling back a beer, stop, take a breath, and observe mindfully. (Wear your watch on the wrong wrist to remind you to be mindful.) Watch as if you're hovering over yourself like a sweet Midol angel. Don't judge the behavior. Just notice who's doing the talking in your head. **Is the voice loving? If the voice is not loving, it's just that curmudgeon Aunt Flow, and she's not you.**

During the week approaching your period, try listening to relaxing music while you meditate, ideally for 20 minutes, twice each day. If you cannot set aside that much time, don't beat yourself up. (Aunt Flow is doing a good job of that already.) Instead, meditate for 10 minutes in the morning, as well as any time you notice you're heading down the rabbit hole. Do a mini-sitting in the shower, in your parked car, during muted commercial breaks on the couch after dinner, and so forth. Meditation isn't complicated. There's really nothing to it.

Sit down, preferably on a hardback chair—it's easier to feel your heartbeat. Close your eyes and breathe. Feel your feelings all the way. Notice where your emotions are landing inside your body. When your mind starts to wander and chit-chat with Aunt Flow, ask her nicely to be quiet so you can focus on your breath and your heartbeat. Sit for 90 seconds then open your eyes and return to your life.

Go ahead and experiment. Try passing your next cycle mindfully and see if it's a little easier. You are your own best teacher. The proof will be in your period.

More

Sometimes it takes a little more than a composed mind to get Flow to step in line. Healing treatments like acupuncture, chiropractic care, and massage open parts of the body that are jammed up, helping you establish natural, healthy rhythms. After receiving about three months of acupuncture, my previously erratic Aunt Flow started arriving quietly and regularly every full moon, like a goddess divine. The night sky replaced my menstrual calendar.

I'm also convinced that this menstrual ease is a divine gift for giving up tampons and pads. I use *The Saalt Cup*, a reusable silicone cup that you insert into the vagina and empty twice a day, and *Thinx*, which are really cute undies that have a washable absorbency pad built into them. My period is carbon clean.

Nooks and crannies happy.

Period drama gone.

Moon

At age 41, I hadn't had sex in almost three years. As a middle-aged woman at the height of my sex drive, I should have been getting it on all the time, but I was partner-less and loveless and not in the mood. My biology was livid and needed answers, so I visited my psychic friend Mary to ask her to ask Archangel Michael if I was lesbian. He said no. I asked her to ask Archangel Raphael if my vagina was broken. Another no. She laughed. The angels laughed. They all agreed that I just needed to get myself out there.

I decided that I should try being slutty. I'd never been slutty before and thought sexual freedom would empower me. I posted a dating profile online and started screening potential lovers. It took me months to vet men through Bumble, a dating app my single friends highly recommended. I had a whole system where I'd build a good list of potential dates then invite them each at staggered times to show up at whatever restaurant my single girlfriends and I were hanging out at. It was fun to meet these men, but no sparks flew, and I remained a born-again virgin. I decided I was too careful to be slutty and just focused on making a genuine connection.

After months of screening, I met a guy who lit me up. We went out for dinner and he walked me to my car where he kissed me like, woah. I mean, *woah*. I hadn't been *woah* kissed in 16 years, so melting into a warm puddle, I thought, *Okay, I'm not lesbian. Maybe bi, but definitely not lesbian.*

About a month later, it was time to giddy-up. I waxed and bathed and beautified. We went for it and it was… awkward. Total bust. We both tried really hard, we just weren't compatible. Without any talk of a next time, we went our separate ways.

The very next evening at moonrise, the time of day made for front porch swings and naps with pets, I sat cross-legged by the window in my empty bedroom. I looked up and glimpsed the narrowest sliver of balsamic moon, closed my eyes and dropped into meditation.

God, thank you for supporting me. Thank you for helping me try to be slutty. Maybe I'll try again someday, but for now, I need to reboot. Please clean me out. Remove any remnants of last night's date from my body and mind. Release us from each other completely and cut all ties that bind us together. Please communicate to him that I have no hard feelings and that our brief relationship was a good learning experience for me.

For about eight years I'd gotten my period every full moon. The next morning, on the first day of the new moon, the goddess Aunt Flow arrived to answer my prayers and clean me out. I had never experienced anything like it. To add to the miracle, the Bumble guy and I disconnected completely and with ease.

The moon and I became besties.

I picked up a book called *Lunar Abundance* by Ezzie Spencer and learned that there's so much more to the moon than menstrual tracking and vaginal care. Each phase radiates a particular energy, alternating between yang energy, which feels assertive and encourages us to get things done, and yin energy, which feels reflective and welcomes us to let things sit. Eight phases support eight specific actions, like setting goals, celebrating nature, and offering gratitude. It's like a guide to using our cosmic superpowers.

When I started doing public talks on the subject, my grandmother warned me that calling on the moon is witchcraft and dangerous, and I should just stick with Jesus. I thought about the grandmothers back in the red tent, the grandmothers of the Bible, celebrating their femininity under the same full moon that hangs over us today, teaching their young girls how to align with the rhythms of nature, using the moon as a cosmic timekeeper. Womankind has strayed too far from our divine nature over centuries of patriarchal miseducation, but I'm happy to see we're returning back to it.

Chapter Summary:

> *May I love my period. May you love your period.*
> *May we love our period.*

When we are mindful, we are simply aware. We are more thoughtful about the food we eat, the comments we make, and the lifestyle choices we make. When we experience our periods mindfully—and especially when we meditate during menses—we create opportunities for our bodies to heal. When we are gentle with our minds, we are more peaceful in our bodies. All of our inner bits are connected, after all.

Journal Prompts:
- Do you track your period on a calendar? If not, please start doing so. Mark the approximate day PMS begins so you can bring extra awareness to your food and drink intake. The day before your period, schedule a nap or an early bedtime.
- How old were you when you got your first period? Were you excited about it? How did its arrival make you feel?
- Did you ever have a traumatic experience with your period? Did that change the way you felt about menstruating?
- Do you like getting a period? Do you use a device or take pills to alter it? Why? Why not?
- What are some of your PMS symptoms? Do other people notice when you're PMS-ing? Do your sensitivities play out in relationships? Who particularly annoys you when you have PMS?
- Have you ever confused yourself with your batty Aunt Flow?

How does it feel to know that you're actually not her? That you are just experiencing a temporary pain-body? Does your perspective shift? Allow you to heal some of your yuck?

7

May I be here, now. May you be here, now. May we be here, now, together.

Stepmonster

By age 25, my big hairy beast and I did almost everything together. You can probably imagine my hesitation when Michael, a man who had an eight-year-old daughter, Chelsea, from a previous marriage, entered my radius. My hairy beast was not interested in shacking up with another person's hairy beast. I came from complicated. I never imagined myself choosing more complicated.

To add to the complication, Michael was 41 when we met. I was 25. I was three years out of college, and he'd already logged 20 years in the workforce. When we went out, people assumed I was Chelsea's babysitter. We were a strange pair. But I liked his big, loving family, his quiet confidence, his easygoing nature, and his interest in protecting and guiding me. Michael, Chelsea, and Chelsea's mom, Nancy, were surprisingly uncomplicated, proving that divorce doesn't break a family; it just restructures it.

He proposed when I was 26 and a year later, I sealed my life with theirs.

Chelsea was chatty and friendly and reminded me of me in many ways. I loved listening to her stories about school and friends and cousins and silliness. I loved reliving my own adventures with her.

As she neared 11, and I neared my wedding nuptials, a part of me turned 11, too. I emotionally morphed into a little girl with bad hair, crooked teeth, and an ill-behaved hairy beast. This 11-year-old Vanessa began to act out through 27-year-old Vanessa.

I felt frantic.

Desperate.

Immature.

Inadequate.

Anxious.

Like my pain and my fears could explode right out of my chest. Was I conscious of why I was doing this at the time?

Absolutely not.

I assumed Chelsea lived with a similar pain as me, with an identical hairy beast. Being a communicator by nature and a journalist by training, I'd ask her zillions of questions and over-share my own heavy feelings about splintered parents and blended families, thinking that I'd help lessen her suffering through my deep, wisdom-y, recently-completed-prefrontal-cortex's understanding of divorce.

I would shuttle her back and forth between her mom and dad, an hour-long car ride, examining her under a lens clouded by fur balls (my beast was a shedder), thinking I was relating and identifying. But really, I was probably just annoying her. The poor thing. My hairy beast sat crammed between us in the front seat during those car rides, as I layered all of my junk on top of her junk.

As it turned out, her beast wasn't anything like mine; and neither of us was better off for my unsolicited unloading. (I'm curling into a little ball of stepmonster shame as I write this.)

Chels and I continued to emotionally mature together. When she turned 13, I turned 13. *OMG, I would tease my hair really high and get all dressed up for school every day...* When she went to summer camp, I went to summer camp. *I loved Camp Hayward! Let me teach you some campfire songs...* When she experienced first love, I experienced first love. *Oh, I remember the first time I held hands with a boy. We were at the movie* Dirty Dancing... Sometimes I judged, *I wouldn't do it that way. You should do it this way...* Sometimes I warned, *Don't make the same mistakes I did...* Sometimes I wished, *Why can't I just shut up?*

My recollections, sometimes benign and sometimes angst-ridden, consistently invited old feelings and dead-end storylines into the present moment; I began to feel small and insecure. I'd wake up from bad dreams about being unhappily married to a mean boy from high school or showing up for tests without pants on. There was one unforgettable night I shot out of bed in a cold sweat after dreaming I was hiding in my childhood closet from a psychotic, gun-wielding version of my father.

Leash

I wasn't sleeping and began passively looking for solutions to heal my thoughts. Sitting on the couch one lazy afternoon with Chelsea, watching television, I flipped to *The Oprah Show*. World-famous psychiatrist Dr. Brian Weiss appeared as her guest, regressing people to past lives through hypnosis. He helped the audience link past life experiences to current life phobias and hang-ups. Together, they dragged past life trauma into the light and transmuted it. Reincarnation resonated immediately as Truth for me. Dr. Weiss provided a spiritual message about oneness, connection, and karma at the exact time I needed to hear it.

That very moment, a path illuminated.

I went to the library and scooped up every Brian Weiss book they had. While my baby girls napped, I laid in bed and listened to his guided regressions on CD, experiencing mental vignettes of my past lives. I was blown away by the lives I saw: a tall, lean black man being shot in the head by a white supremacist in Chicago; an ancient Chinese woman dying in a tiny house, alone but happy; a little white country girl and her twin sister, whom I felt was Nancy, running in a meadow; an old goat herder in Nepal who died on a mountain and was buried under a pile of rocks by his devoted daughter. My brain became a fascinating place. I wanted to do more with my mind and sought meditation techniques.

In 2008, when I was exploring these techniques, meditation wasn't hot like it is now. I struggled to find a teacher. YouTube had one grainy meditation video; it was three minutes long and featured a bearded white guy saying "So hum" over and over. I returned to the library and checked out books by Thich Nhat Hahn, Chogyam Trungpa, and Jon Kabat-Zinn. Eventually I hooked into a weekly meditation sitting at Cambridge Insight Meditation Center, and then another weekly dharma talk at a local Tibetan Buddhism center.

Meditation had officially become a practice for me.

And then, while sitting one day, a tiny, beautiful shift happened. In a moment of grace, I recognized my habitual emotional pattern. I noticed that the progressive reappearance of my youth's emotional landscape matched pace with Chelsea's maturation. I noticed that my insecurity and nightmares were triggered by our conversations. I responded by forgiving myself for accidentally regressing to this life's childhood trauma and finally slept soundly.

For the first time ever, I leashed the beast.

Yah baby.

It wasn't easy to keep him under control. At first, the beast would tug and pull on the leash, cutting me off, running ahead of me, trying to jump on people in his path. He'd drag me off running with my hurt-little-girl or bitchy-teenager emotions, ready to attack people, defending something that didn't need defending. But I was vigilant in taming him, using meditation to help me stay tuned in. I'd watch my beast watching the world, see him twitch and salivate, and tug him close before he started wreaking havoc.

With patience and practice, he walked beside me, and then eventually a few steps behind.

From time to time, he'd still spot something tempting in our periphery and dart out ahead of me. Be it with great gusto or invisible effort, I could always tighten that leash and reel him back to his place, imploring him to keep his fur balls and drool to himself.

If you're into self-help, you probably recognize that the hairy beast (like IBS and Aunt Flow) is what enlightenment teacher Eckhart Tolle might call a *pain-body*. The pain-body is a protective emotional construct that pretends to be you but is not you. The leash (like the *Maasdam* and the red tent) is distance. Distance creates space between you and the pain-body's miscreation. Distance allows us fresh perspective so that we can get back on our feet and survey what is *actually* happening rather than what we *think* is happening.

We saw how moving away provided me with physical distance from a problem and gave space to heal; but moving away is not a reasonable solution for most. We can create emotional distance in the mind through meditation. This formal practice of watching thoughts invites us to play the role of silent witness. From a place of neutrality, we separate ourselves from our experience and observe without judging or wishing or rewriting. Instead, we apply compassion and curiosity.

Remember, your yuck cannot be kept hidden—especially from your kids. No matter how much you'd like to believe that your beast is your problem, this just isn't true. That hairy pain-in-the-ass touches every person you meet. Then those people touch other people with little pieces of your yuck.

The upside is that your love touches everyone, too.

By getting control over your own complicated, messy, hairy beast, you are not only improving the quality of your own life, but the lives of everyone you connect with directly or indirectly. And one day, while comforting your ostracized seventh grader or strolling past a neighborhood barbeque you weren't invited to, you'll watch without internalizing, and you will smile with gratitude that your efforts are working. Everyone you know will benefit from your peace of mind.

Generations

Healing won't drop out of the sky. You must want it, seek it, and sometimes fight for it. **If you want to heal, you need to decide to heal and work hard to make it happen.** Vigilance is the way. (Buddhists might call this *right effort*.) Vigilance is the determination and consistency required to see bullshit for what it is and distance yourself from it. Mindfulness doesn't exist without your commitment, discipline, and willingness.

This verse is written in The Dhammapada, a collection of Buddhist scripture:

> *Whatever a mother, father*
> *Or other relative may do,*
> *Far better is the benefit*
> *From one's own rightly directed mind.*
> *Dhammapada 43*

I interpret this verse in two ways, and I think both are important in separating from generational dogma. First, we parents can coach and direct and lecture, but the best wisdom our children can generate is that from their own experience. We have to let them do them.

Second, there comes a point when we as parents can no longer relive *our* parents' mistakes or continue to pass on *their* poor choices. It's healthy to let go of limitations and traditions that no longer serve and to step into our personal alignment. Many ancient religions and wisdom traditions say that our personal healing reaches seven generations back and seven generations forward.

Our efforts matter.

I need to ensure you, right now, that there is a path that leads away from suffering. And every time you choose wholesome, loving action, you thin out the cord that connects you to your painful emotional past. There's a whole lotta story between that beast-leashing episode and my life now, but if we can fast forward to today for just a moment, I want to inject a spoiler alert.

I'm a normal person. Decidedly un-special. Absolutely imperfect. But because I chose love and continue to choose love— over and over and over again—my hairy beast is no longer a leashed companion. I imagine that he lives deep in the forest, skipping among tall oak trees, wearing a garland of white daisies on his head.

In the end, because I was vigilant in using mindfulness and meditation to leash the beast, when Chelsea went to prom, I didn't go to prom. I snapped a few photos and complimented her gorgeous dress. When she applied to colleges, I didn't apply to colleges. I supported her application process from a distance and applauded her acceptance to her top pick, University of Miami. When she got her first job, I didn't get my first job. I took her shopping for skirts and blazers at Ann Taylor. With Chelsea's wedding plans underway and likely babies soon to come, I will have plenty of opportunities to practice mindful parenting, plenty of opportunities to stay true to my emotional and spiritual integrity, and plenty of opportunities to benefit generations past and future.

Chapter Summary:

> *May I be here, now. May you be here, now.*
> *May we be here, now, together.*

Isn't it crazy to discover all the ways childhood trauma can manifest in your adult life? Geez Louise! The now moment can get pretty fuzzy sometimes, especially as our kids' lives unfold in painfully familiar ways. As a parent, reliving aspects of your youth is inevitable, but it's absolutely imperative that you remember these two things: one, you are not that girl anymore; and two, your child is not you. I'm not saying anything you don't already know, just cheering on that little voice in your head that's telling you you're okay… and you should probably stop talking.

Journal Prompts:
- What's the deal with your beast? How and when does he show up for you as an adult?
- Is your beast the result of an explicit memory or do you have to dig into implicit memories to find his origins?
- Have you ever paused to congratulate yourself on leashing a beast? For healing an old trauma?
- How do you acknowledge or commemorate your healing? Talk about it with friends? Record the insight in a journal? Take a selfie of the evolved new you? Do you think recording the healing even matters?

8

May I have fun. May you have fun. May we have fun.

Yuck

Scarlett arrived 22 months after Penelope. Born on Father's Day, she was an angel baby—beautiful, healthy, happy. Despite the easy infant and gorgeous weather, contending with two tiny night-wakers was torture on my energy and focus. To make matters more challenging, my thyroid had tanked after my first pregnancy. Drastically changing hormones made it hard for my doctor to ascertain the right medication levels to regulate my thyroid, which exhausted me. While sluggishly hoisting the girls out of their cribs each morning, I'd already be anticipating their naptime and my next chance to catch up on zzz's.

My mind slacked. I'd fold laundry and get lost in old memories; lie on the floor and daydream while the girls played with blocks; listen to endless hours of NPR while washing floors and counters, then immediately forget the stories. I was not as present as I could have been with my baby girls—or even with myself. I was just too sleepy.

If I'm to be honest here, I wasn't happy either. Jennifer Senior wrote a modern parenting book called *All Joy and No Fun*. That title pretty much summed up my feelings about being a young mom. Watching my babies discover the world was like watching a miracle unfold. Joy came in the form of awe and amazement. It filled up my heart. But fun? I lost track of that. While my heart was robust, my brain was about the consistency of rice cereal mixed with breast milk.

To me, fun was about learning and building things, working on creative projects with colleagues, having intellectual conversations, organizing people, coming up with clever solutions, traveling and exploring, playing strategic games. Young motherhood provided very little of that, and consequently, the fun part of me went dormant.

This is not to say I didn't enjoy tickling my babies under their waddle-y chins, playing *Pretty Pretty Princess* seven times a day, and giving them underdogs on park swings. I happily did all those sweet mommy things and more, but my kind of fun was elusive. I sensed that the experiences I craved were embedded in my life purpose,[6] only I didn't know what that purpose was or how I could even search for it while caring for the girls.

When we got engaged, Michael and I decided that I'd stay home with any children we'd produce. It seems strange now, making a decision like that when I was just 26. I had only recently finished school, was burning up with entrepreneurial ideas, and had no clue what it meant to be a mother. We assumed I'd be content to push my career dreams to the back burner, assumed that the responsibility of motherhood would naturally override or perhaps even erase any other calling. It's the story of a billion women, but it's a strange assumption all the same. Idealistic. Normative. Un-insightful.

Without understanding why, as a stay-at-home mom with two

---

[6]I kind of hate the phrase "life purpose" and actually bristled while writing it. There is far too much pressure on people to figure out their life purpose. The purpose of life is to be happy. Your divine assignment may be just to exist here and experience Earth as it awakens.

little adorable, playful, perfect little girls, I was chronically irritated. Smiles were saved for public interactions. By the time Scarlett was 18 months, I found myself spiraling toward depression—a familiar condition for me.

I remember watching Michael one cold Saturday morning; he seemed to have not a care in the world, reading *The Wall Street Journal*, sipping coffee, relaxing in an overstuffed chair with the sun streaming down on him through the window. Across the room, I scrubbed the stovetop and scowled at him from under furrowed brows. I think I was growling, literally. *What are you so friggin' happy about?* I seethed.

Yuck, right?

Though I worked hard not to acknowledge it, misery seeped out of me and rippled out to my family and friends, like dark Metta. Penelope, who was almost three at the time, peered at me from across the kitchen island and peeped, "Momma? Why don't you ever smile?" After six-and-a-half minutes of choking on sobs, I swallowed my last tear and peeled my mascara-stained face off the granite countertop, promising, "I don't know, P. I'm so sorry. I'm going to figure out how to smile more."

Penelope's compassionate curiosity forced me to see myself from her perspective. Another tiny shift jerked me awake. I needed a way to get better.

I needed an outlet.

Outlet

Writing was a lifelong love of mine, a natural way to explore life, but I'd been so consumed by the yuck that I never thought to reach for a pen. I reached past Penelope and grabbed an envelope from a nearby stack of mail and began scratching out thoughts on the back of it. Over days and weeks to follow, I'd sit with the girls during craft time; while they colored, I scribbled poems and mapped out fictional plots. Then one evening after putting the girls to sleep, I dug an old diary from my bedside table and leafed to a blank page. I wrote and I wrote and I wrote. And I cried and I cried and I cried. I couldn't stop writing and crying — about my pain, about my sadness, about my kids, about my husband, about my father, about my confusion, about my past, about my future, about my God. The words poured out of me until I fell asleep with the light on, on a bed of crumpled pages.

The next day I woke up and reread what I wrote. It was beautiful. I remembered I had talent, that I was a trained journalist, that I had a gift. *Oh my goodness, I had a gift!*

The ritual of writing made me feel less crazy, so I continued.

A gorgeous release of ink and emotion took place each time I slashed a diary page with my pen. The dramatic loops of letters and inky slices were equivalent to punching a pillow. I had discovered my first *spiritually based mental health practice*. It felt amazing.

Slashing and slicing weren't always what I needed, though. When I wanted to open up my heart space or find inspiration, typing on a keyboard was fast and enabled me to channel voices much wiser than my own. (The inspiration didn't slip past while dotting i's and crossing t's.) My fingers often produced a mix of jibberish and love, which eventually I learned was automatic writing:

blah blah blah blah blah blah blah blah blah this is so boring i am so bored why i am i doing this what am i doing i am wondering what can come from this just move just listen You are light sweet child. You are light and love. Listen to your heart and you will always have the answers.

Not very fancy or eloquent. Sometimes words came through all poetry and loveliness, sometimes the message only made sense to me. Just like a sitting meditation—whatever it was, was what it was.

The more I wrote, the more I wanted to write. The more I poked at big questions and feelings, the more I revealed truths that guided me toward purpose. I heard the quietest parts of myself over the tapping of keys, and recorded my life's history, not from the viewpoint of a confused, rejected child, but from the viewpoint of a compassionate, wise woman. I wrote myself out of the damsel in distress role and explored the idea of playing the superhero.

The effort took years and every draft mattered. Each iteration was a turning of the aperture, bringing clarity to events in my life that felt out of focus. The process challenged me creatively and artistically. Writing made me feel powerful, productive, and purposeful.

I was finally having fun.

My brain felt placated.

As an added bonus, the practice provided me yet another tiny shift in perspective. I remembered the person I had started becoming before having babies. I published my first blog and was invited to be a columnist for my local newspaper. As heart and head aligned, even mothering became more fun for me.

Woot

Fun is a concept in healing that no one ever talks about. Often times when we heal, the process is associated with some type of mental or physical discomfort—boot camp, shock therapy, acupuncture needles, pills with nasty side effects... these are healing modalities we've all subscribed to, and while they are helpful, they're not exactly "fun." In fact, often times the healing techniques we engage feel like chores. Oh, how we dread chores! Perhaps that's why so many people resist self-work?

My advice to those interested in healing old wounds and raising their vibration is this: take something you have fun doing and elevate it to a spiritually based mental health practice, like I did with writing. For example, if you love to cook, make serving your family healthy meals your path to ascension. Let the food guide your journey. Invite friends to cook with you. Eat mindfully. Find the metaphors reflecting between your spiritual life and your food life and write them all down.

Are you an athlete? Weave mindfulness into your daily conditioning. Get fit in nature. Honor your temple with a gentle yoga practice. Hike with someone who inspires you. Play games without keeping score.[7] Journal about connections you make between your body, mind, and spirit.

Regardless of the way you have fun healing your yuck, it's important to record the experience and the parallels. If you're a writer like me, you probably have a strong journaling practice and are familiar with the catharses that arise from this exercise. Automatic writing, a process during which your higher self pours through your pen, is an effective way to dig up the roots of your suffering. If you've never done it, let's have some fun and end this chapter shockingly abruptly so you can write. Put this book down, grab a notebook and pen, and take a seat.

Close your eyes and focus on breath: in through your nose, the belly rises; out through your nose, the belly falls. Spend a couple minutes tuning into the rhythm of your breath, noises in the room, sensations in your body. Ask a question, the first one that comes to mind. Put pen to paper and start writing. See what happens. Don't

---

[7]There is nothing spiritually healthy about competition—gasp!—so reframe your goals and take your athleticism to a higher level by playing collaboratively.

think, just write.

Chapter Summary:

May I have fun. May you have fun. May we have fun.

Have you ever tried writing your personal history from today's perspective? Try it now. Perhaps after you've finished writing, you'll feel better. Perhaps you'll feel worse. Perhaps you'll feel exhausted. It's all okay. Sit with the feelings. Make thoughtful connections. Find the old trauma and connect it to today's trigger. And then maybe, maybe, maybe see the lesson in it. Acknowledge the beauty that grows from the pain, the lotus that grows from the mud. Write that down, too. Notice your hands loosening up. Notice how your clutch around the pen changes. Record any feelings of gratitude, any peaceful action you can take, any to-do's that are based in self-care. Try to elevate your mindset through this exercise by ending on a positive note. This creates a new path that your mind can follow. This path may even be fun to explore.

Journal Prompts:
- What does fun mean to you? Are you having it? If not, think back to yourself as a kid and young adult. What was fun back then? Could those activities be relevant now?
- Do you have current spiritual practices that you consider fun? For example, I love being in nature. It brings me peace and connection. It soothes my heart. Fun feels different. It energizes my brain, makes me laugh. Journey Dance, a spiritual dance practice created by my friend Toni Bergins, is FUN. It's like shamanism meets Justin Timberlake.
- What do you think about heart vs. head? Is there a difference?

- What is the most profound piece of insight you have collected through journaling?

9

May I have peace of mind. May you have peace of mind. May we have peace of mind.

Sit

Writing is just one of a zillion types of meditation that can help you make healing connections and draw forward the best parts of yourself. You can also use mantras or objects, sounds or music, breath or nature. You can watch birds build a nest or listen to ocean waves. You can use nothing at all and just bear witness to your mind as it wanders here, there, and everywhere. When my mind is super squirrely, focusing on the tip of my nose works well. I don't know why it's such a powerful approach for me, but why question peace of mind?

If a squirrely mind makes your body crave movement, try a meditative walk or jog. Use your sneakers on the pavement as an anchor, allowing focus to rest on the connection between your body and the earth. When your mind wanders, bring it back to your padding feet. You could even consider sewing, knitting, playing piano, or fixing cars as a type of meditation, so long as you're not attached to outcomes and you are 100% focused on your neutral experience of the task.

If you're this far into the book and still have never meditated before, go ahead and try it right now.

Give yourself five minutes. Set a timer, then close your eyes and take five deep breaths; in through the nose, out through the mouth. Then close your mouth and begin to count your breaths. In and out is one. See if you can get to 10 or 15. If you get lost, just start over again from one. Notice where each inhale lands in the body, becoming aware of the way the back and chest, or belly and waist expand. Then notice the opposite on your exhale, a slight contraction in and up of the belly, warm air exiting the nose, a slight drop of the shoulders. If your mind is wandering all over the place, don't give up. This is totally normal. Acknowledge the thoughts coming in, perhaps labeling them "thoughts." If you can't make the full five minutes, it's okay. Open your eyes, come back to this book, and try to meditate another time.

This is meditation. Posture is important, especially during long sittings, but I often tell first time students to just sit comfortably. If you're comfortable, you're more likely to do it again.

Meditating for 20 minutes, twice a day is the recommended dose. I know people who do 10-20 minutes of mantra work (see next section) in the morning and bookend the day with something less structured, like a sound meditation. Andy Puddicomb of *Headspace* fame suggests 10 minutes a day; his downloadable app is helpful for people who benefit from guidance. Remember, though, you are the expert in your life. Choose time increments that work for you.

You may notice that even after a one-minute meditation you feel more relaxed. You may notice the first transitional moments into your sitting feel weird or awkward. Or you may notice that your mind wanders a lot. The wandering is an important part of the practice. As soon as you notice a stray thought you engage awareness, at which point you can choose to either follow the thought mindfully or release the thought and return to observing or counting your breath. In this way, you become not lost in thought, but found in it.

Sometimes when my mind is really jacked up, I'll sit for five minutes and suffer all the way through. Maintaining focus for the duration of one breath feels like doing a bicep curl with a 90-pound weight. Other times, I can focus on breath for a whole hour with barely a whisper of effort, like curling a pencil. Both are acceptable because both require effort. It's that simple.

Repeat

If breath work is not your jam, try using a mantra. A mantra is a short phrase or a single word, repeated over and over as a way to transcend thought. It is perfect for beginner meditators, especially those who have trouble relaxing or sleeping and those who are healing the physical body. It is not the best tool for deep insight, but it's an awesome way to get in "the zone" quickly or befriend a budding meditation practice. People often use Sanskrit words as mantras, but you can choose any word that does not evoke an emotional charge.

When you sit down to practice mantra-based meditation, take five deep breaths, in through the nose and out through the mouth, just to get your mind and body settled. When you're comfortable, begin repeating the mantra silently, at your own pace. When the mind wanders away from the mantra, gently invite the mind to return to the repetition.

In this type of meditation, we do not follow stray thoughts, but we don't kick them to the curb either. We become aware of the wandering, acknowledge the thought, then compassionately return to the mantra. The trick of the mantra is to make it louder than your thoughts. Start loud, then play with the volume of the mantra, slowly letting it diminish as the body and mind chill out. When noisy thoughts pop up, turn the volume back up then patiently repeat the mantra as the body and mind settle again.

There are a bunch of things that will happen when you use a mantra. You'll repeat just the mantra; you'll notice thoughts without any mantra; you'll notice thoughts and mantra happening together; you'll fall asleep; you'll feel relaxed; your breath will get so shallow you'll take a sudden deep breath; you'll feel twitchy; you'll get bored; you'll experience the space of no thought and no mantra, also called "the gap."

Some funky things can also happen while using mantra (or really any other kind of meditation practice), for example seeing visions, colors, patterns, or shapes; experiencing feelings of floating, largeness, or all-over tingles; hearing voices or smelling scents; losing sense of space and time; traveling outside of your body, perhaps into the cosmos or other lifetimes; interacting with ethereal beings; spontaneously healing aspects of your human body and mind; adopting a wholly new outlook on a situation or person; and tapping into omniscience.

So how do you pick a mantra? You can pay a lot of money and receive a mantra from a Transcendental Meditation teacher. I did that. But TM training isn't necessary to engage a mantra-based practice. There are several classic Sanskrit mantras you can work with. *So hum* is an easy one. It means "I am." Deepak Chopra and Oprah Winfrey offer dozens of mantras on their guided meditation recordings and pair them with inspiring dharma talks. You can buy these recordings online or wait until they come out with the next cycle of free meditation experiences.

Think of mantra-based meditation, or any meditation approach, like going for an early summer swim in the ocean. The first step in can be a frigid shock, uncomfortable. As a lifelong New Englander, I know all about cold water. On the south shore of Massachusetts, where I grew up, a June dip in the Atlantic would typically come to an abrupt end when my mom called, "Your lips are blue, Vanessa! Time to get out!" That water turned me into an ice pop, but damn, I had so much fun playing in it. Eventually I'd give myself over to the chill and just play, aware of the cold and the current but not distracted or disturbed by it.

During meditation, use stillness in the same way. Though it may feel uncomfortable at first, with determination and discipline you will acclimate, and the stillness—like the cold—will become a place where you can explore comfortably.

After those chilly swims, I'd shiver, shake, and chatter my way up the beach, covered in goose bumps, hopping from foot to foot while I reached for a towel. After bundling myself in terrycloth, Mom would warm me up with a tender hug.

Releasing a meditation can feel the same way. So, emerge gently from stillness, wrap yourself in loving kindness. Perhaps this means you take a moment to place your hand over your heart in gratitude. Maybe you wipe tears away and drink a glass of water. Maybe you just sit and let your mind wander for a few minutes, taking inventory of new insight. Maybe you high five yourself, excited about a new burst of creativity. Maybe you sit back and look around, absorbing your surroundings with fresh eyes and renewed perspective. Or maybe, just like you would after an early summer swim, you give yourself a big hug.

Walk

I'm going to cheat and dip into the *Then Your Family* section for the remainder of this chapter on experiencing peace of mind, just because the time feels right.

As we establish a strong mindfulness and meditation practice, it's natural to want to teach the kids, but this may not be an easy task. *We* may love sitting in meditation, but it's not for everyone. The practice enthralls some and repels others. I had an adult student once who stood up and screamed at the conclusion of her first sitting. No lie. She gave stillness the finger and sprinted out of class.

If sitting quietly in meditation makes you, your kids, or your students want to press the emergency eject button, try a walking meditation. This is not a speed walking meditation; there is no element of exercise. Steps should be slow and deliberate, with minimal exertion. The intention is to observe the movements and sensations in the body as well as thoughts and feelings that arise as we wander. Walking meditation is also a wonderful opportunity to take our practice off the mat and integrate it into real life.

In his book *Planting Seeds*, Thich Nhat Hanh teaches walking meditation like a fun game. I've had tremendous success with his technique. Have your kids line up behind you and direct them to walk slowly, paying attention to their feet as they walk. *Which muscles are moving? Do your arms stop moving naturally when you think about them? Is it hard to balance when you walk this slowly?* Then ask them to walk like a robot, like a cat burglar, like a monkey. Walk like they're on the moon, in knee-deep snow. Walk like they're listening to their favorite song. Walk super-duper fast. *What do you notice? Which way is the loudest? Which way is quietest? Which way makes you breathe heavy?*

My crew and I did this activity one September Sunday on the town green. The next thing I knew, six extra kids had hopped into my line and started practicing mindful walking with us. I'd suddenly become the mindful Pied Piper.

Unplug

Screens are the default babysitter for most parents. When we need the kids to be quiet, we chuck a tablet at them or turn on the TV, creating budding screenagers. Of course, we adults are equally guilty of screen addiction. Electronics distract us from true peace of mind.

My childhood friend, Janell Burley-Hofmann, wrote *iRules*, a book about raising kids who respect technology, and I recommend it for anyone longing to create mindful boundaries around gadgets, screens, and social media. Technology is constantly changing, and so are our children; it's okay to change the rules without notice. Janell and I both practice empowered parenting. In other words, if something is happening at home that's not working, we grant ourselves full permission to restructure, renegotiate, or retreat.

Tech becomes a problem in my household when I get lazy about parenting it. When Xavi was eight, I noticed that a thick layer of dust was forming over his dragon and knight figurines. I couldn't remember the last time I saw him playing imaginatively. He had become so reliant on screens and tech that when I set up a battle scene on his bedroom floor, he shrugged and asked to watch *Slugterra* on Netflix instead. When I said no, he freaked, and I knew it was time to restructure the rules. The screens had to go.

I know my younger kids can go months without gadgets, so long as I lock them up (the gadgets, not the kids). But when their stuff is hidden away and I am attached to my iPhone, they salivate. They steal it, they hide in corners with it, they beg for it. My solution? I unplug, too. The disconnect forces me into the real world and we all benefit from the unstructured time together. We eventually surrender to spontaneity, imagination, and the magic of boredom.

A word of warning: the first two weeks of tech removal are brutal. For our addicted little Minecraft monkeys, it's like quitting meth cold turkey. You may want to plan the first week of detox around a rehab-style vacation to soothe the transition.

Un-plan

Boredom is a rock star way to cultivate creativity, which allows kids to express themselves artistically and access peace. True, you'll have to suffer through, "Mommy, I'm bored. What can I do?" 16 times before the kids settle into a project; but it's a terrific opportunity to remind them, "It's okay to be bored. You're creative. You'll figure something out."

They always do figure it out, so you've just scored a well-deserved point in the Mommy's Usually Right category. And while they're inventing a new gizmo or directing a home movie, you can smile and watch them play—or you can meditate, read a book, paint a picture, organize a closet, or simply stare out a window.

If you're brave enough to further protect their free time by reducing their scheduled activities, you'll experience the added bonus of not having to rush out the door for drop-offs and pick-ups. You can relax into your own self-care experience. When your kids see you take care of yourself, they honor that need for themselves. So set your crew *and yourself* up for success by *un*-planning ahead of time.

Eat

Whether you're serving up cereal or salmon, mealtime is made for mindfulness. Mindful meal planning took on new meaning after I heard about a 2016 University of Chicago study in which two women, Kaitlin Woolley and Ayelet Fishback, found that eating the same food as another person can promote trust and cooperation by increasing closeness and liking. They discovered that strangers who ate the same food were able to resolve issues more quickly than people who ate different foods, calling the experience of shared flavor a "social lubricant." Wild, right? So if you're slinging food like a short order cook at dinnertime, put on the breaks. Find a couple of family-style meal solutions that will work for everyone and see how your brood responds.

Once you sit down to eat together, welcome awareness and wholesome intention. Saying grace before a meal is common practice in American households and a beautiful way to come together, mindfully and spiritually. In my family, we join hands and say an adapted Thich Nhat Hanh prayer, "My plate is filled with food, and with each bite I practice loving kindness."

During the meal, see if you can keep your conversation centered on the present moment by inviting your kids to pretend that they're aliens seeing food for the first time. Have them describe what they see, taste, feel, hear, and smell. You could also challenge them to talk only about things that are happening now. It's surprisingly difficult!

Chapter Summary:

> *May I have peace of mind. May you have peace of mind.*
> *May we have peace of mind.*

This chapter is about finding ways to practice meditation and mindfulness that meet you where you are. It's very possible that none of these techniques work for you, but that doesn't mean you are not worthy of stillness or peace of mind. Keep searching! You will find reward in the effort.

Journal Prompts:

- I have just one loaded question: What holds you back from committing to a meditation practice? (Time is not a valid answer.)

10

May I be aware. May you be aware. May we be aware.

Intersection

People often ask me what the difference is between mindfulness and meditation. Here is how I differentiate them: Meditation is a formal, intentional practice with one point of focus and a clear start and finish. The practice is connected to stillness, though that stillness may not be physical, as in a practice like Tai Chi. Tai Chi, while based in movement, is still concentrated and singularly focused, and is therefore a meditation.

Mindfulness is attending with your fullness of presence, taking the world in through your senses with intense awareness, perhaps even feeling your place in the Universe and letting *it* work through *you*. It can be more than observation; it can be total trust. Mindfulness is an informal practice, without a start or a finish, a living meditation, an opportunity to live above one's conditioning.

Mindfulness and meditation are secular, scientifically supported practices appropriate for people of all races, religions, and cultures. They can be taught in public schools, doctors' offices, and capitol buildings. These practices can be engaged by scientists, Christians, Muslims, atheists, doctors, capitalists, and Bieber fans. Science assures the world that there are no spiritual attachments to this practice.

However.

I personally find it impossible to clearly define where the science ends and the spiritual begins. Because I'm not writing a godless textbook, I'm going to lay this out the way I see it. To me, meditation is the very intersection of humanness and holiness. It's a clear path between my head, my heart, and my two bunioned feet that helps me to release some of the heaviness that builds up while living life here on Earth. When my body and mind are less dense, the purest part of my being—my spirit—can shine through more easily and I simply feel happier.

A practice like this takes time and commitment to establish, but it's well worth the effort. Vijaya Lakshmi Pandit, India's first woman to be appointed a cabinet position, said, "The more we sweat in peace, the less we bleed in war." The vigilance we offer to our peace practice may not end our ongoing internal war—everyone who is alive knows suffering—but it sure helps us manage the battles intrinsic in being a human, and specifically a parent. When we are in our right mind, we remain composed with our challenging children. We see clearly. We think in solutions. We access sound responses. We expand compassion. We aren't flawless, but we are composed. We're less burdened. And when we're less burdened, there's more headspace for spirit to work its way through. Here's how:

Modern science and technology spell out the link between meditation and neural composure, using brain scans and research studies to confirm what mystics and monks have understood intuitively for millennia. If you are picking up this book, chances are you're aware of the copious research on ways meditation and mindfulness can benefit our brains. A quick online search will connect you to dozens of viable research studies, like Sarah Lazar's viral 2011 study, performed by academic and medical institutions around the world. These studies will agree that the brain is *neuroplastic*, which basically means that the brain's neural pathways are constantly reshaping themselves in response to the way they're stimulated. Studies will also confirm that meditation inspires measurable growth in the brain's white matter, creating stronger connections between areas that control executive function, emotional regulation, memory, cognition, fear, and more. These structural changes improve the composition and flexibility of our thoughts, helping us to be more loving, creative, compassionate, composed, assured human beings.

How does a restructured brain make us better people? Better parents? Can it shorten our commutes or remind our kids to flush the toilet? Will it annihilate our arthritis pain or guide us to winning lottery numbers? How do these subtle shifts in neurology play out in the harder-to-measure parts of our lives? How do they reduce our stress?

Simply put, stress is resistance to what *is*. The rush hour traffic, the stack of bills, the aching joints, the ailing parents… these circumstances make us feel emotionally messy, not because the *experiences* are charged, but because *we* are. We are charged with a notion that our circumstances should be different, warmer, healthier, easier to navigate, more transparent. That charge makes us squirm and squirming makes the yuck rise, clouding our thoughts while we perform tasks like housework and carpools, tasks that have nothing to do with the yuck. (We'll call out the hormone behind this charge in chapter 15.)

When our minds are focused and quiet, we generate a meditative stillness that settles the yuck and clears the way for those new neural pathways. These pathways are made of alternatives, creative solutions, improved health, and insight on various outcomes. This perspective can help prepare us for the unexpected. Being prepared for the unexpected reduces our stress, the thing that perpetuates our suffering. Reduced stress yields peace of mind, and peace of mind leaves all sorts of space for God's Love to inch in. It's the Love that lifts our vibration, not necessarily the biology.

Costas

My favorite teacher Thich Nhat Hanh might say mindfulness is doing the dishes and knowing we're doing the dishes. It's meditation in action. But how do we *just* do the dishes when we're doing the dishes? Because most of the time, while we're doing the dishes, we're thinking about what an asshole our boss is or how much our back hurts when we lean over the sink.

Here's my suggestion: ***Don't ruminate. Commentate***. Empower your inner Bob Costas. Pretend you're a sportscaster giving a play-by-play on dishwashing:

A wave of silence washes over the mind as Vanessa steps up to the sink, plants her feet, takes a breath. She examines the mess: four dirty grilled cheese plates, one knife, six small cups, and an ice cream scoop. She turns on the tap, feeling grateful for such easy access to hot water, adjusts her stance, softens her knees, rolls up her sleeves, and reaches for a glass. Vanessa spots a subtle fuchsia lipstick stain, picks up a warm, bubbly sponge, and begins to scrub...

Sometimes while you're doing the dishes, you're not ruminating, you're reminiscing. You're scrubbing and thinking about a pleasant day you had at the beach with your family or the fabulous sex you had with your partner last night. Maybe you're projecting into the future, anticipating a fun party or vacation you've been planning for weeks. The thoughts that you would typically classify as "good" are important to watch, too. Just like the "bad" thoughts, they keep you from experiencing this moment.

Here, now.

They are all distractions to your peace of mind, your productivity, and your clarity.

This practice of commentating keeps you firmly grounded in the present moment because you cannot commentate and ruminate (or daydream or reminisce) at the same time. But again, we must *remember* to do it. Let's brainstorm a few practical ways we can use our environment to support a practice by stimulating memory and activating awareness all day long. These tools are especially helpful for folks who dip in and out of depression, like *moi*.

- Let the color yellow engage your practice. When you see yellow, give yourself a compliment. (Any color will work. I just like yellow.)
- Draw a heart on the back of your hand with a Sharpie. Smile when you notice it.
- Wear your watch on the wrong wrist. Feel it and make a good decision.
- Put a neon collar on your dog. Love and be loved.
- Paint your kitchen light switch turquoise. Flick it and turn on your inner light.
- See the letter B. Be here, now.
- Program *Jump in the Line* by Harry Belafonte as your ringtone. Get a call and shake, shake, shake, Señora.
- Choose a "word of the day." Hear it, stop, take one mindful breath.
- Wear mismatched socks. Every time you cross your legs, remember to smile.
- Search for Mini Coopers on the road. See one and loosen your grip on the wheel.

- Paint your toenails in rainbow colors. Look down and feel happy.
- Buy or cut flowers for your home every week. Stop to smell them.

Start by introducing just one of these ideas. Once you get used to responding to it, add more yuck to transmute. Within a few weeks or months, you'll be breathing and smiling and loving at multiple triggers—or maybe you'll be noticing that you're not breathing or smiling or loving. If that's the case, you may find yourself ready to understand why you're not, at which point you can try meditating on the roots of love and pain in your life.

Runneth

Think of each breath as an invitation to reestablish your mind in the one truly healthy place that exists: the present moment. For the first few years I practiced mindfulness, I didn't really "get" breath. I understood it solely as a convenient practice tool. After many years of practicing, my relationship with breath is much changed. Now I understand that each inhale is a reunion with God. Each exhale is a release of collaborative intention into the world around me.

At eight breaths a minute, we have 11,520 opportunities a day to experience this divine collaboration. The question is: how will we show up when God is standing at our threshold? Will we be distracted by the yuck? Daydreaming about the future? Or will we be attentive in the present? Through mindfulness practices, we train our brain to rest in the only place God can be experienced: now.

Having all these opportunities to raise our vibration is happy news for us, and happier news for our kids; after all, they're first in line to suffer the effects of our suffering. When our cup runneth over with Love, they are first in line to receive that, too.

Metta, baby. Metta.

Chapter Summary:

May I be aware. May you be aware. May we be aware.

Meditation will not solve the world's problems, you will. Meditating does not automatically mean you are kind, smart, wise, or well-intended. **Meditation is not a magic pill, it's an open door.** It's an opportunity for you to choose how you'd like to grow and heal. Stillness is the ideal condition for growth and healing.

Once, when Scarlett had the flu, she asked, "Mom, why do I need to lay down and drink tea when I'm sick?"

I said, "If we plant a seedling in a terra cotta pot and want it to grow into something beautiful, do we shake the pot all day?" She shook her head. "Do we scream and yell, 'Oh my goodness! A leaf on the plant is withering! This is a disaster! Someone do something!'" She smiled and shook her head again. "Of course not," I said. "We leave it be. When the plant is still, it has more energy to grow straight and tall. We never need to worry about the plant because healing is its natural state, we just need to make sure it's in a supportive environment and gets plenty of sunlight and water."

That's really what you're trying to do through this practice: create ideal conditions for your maximum potential fulfillment, moment by moment.

Journal Prompts:
- When we start teaching concepts, we really start to understand them. Explain in your own words what happens in the brain when you meditate. Then teach one of your kids.
- What are you typically doing when you get totally lost in

thought? Driving? Doing chores? Jogging? Trying to get to sleep? Come up with an environmental trigger that will remind you to commentate your way through mentally slack moments. Then buy it, make it, or create it right away.

- Describe a time you overreacted to something. Now describe how that experience could have unfolded had you remembered that you are a compassionate, loving, mindful human being. Don't judge. Just imagine.

11

May I forgive and be happy. May you forgive and be happy. May we forgive and be happy.

Forgiveness

The day that Penelope asked, "Mommy, why don't you ever smile?" I was stunned. *Do I really never smile? When was the last time I laughed? When was the last time I felt joy? Oh my God. I can't remember. I can't remember! I CAN'T REMEMBER!!!!*

I panicked.

I bawled.

Penelope's words stung me over and over and over. Have you ever had a yellow jacket stuck in your shorts? I have. It felt like that, but in my heart. And I knew right then that I was alive, and even if only to her, that I mattered. I wanted to wake up from my secret depression, my secret shame. I wanted to feel good, to be happy.

Writing and meditating helped me feel purposeful and connected, but deep-seated joy still eluded. This was so frustrating! I'd been doing the right things, I'd studied my self-help books, I'd connected neural pathways and reduced stress levels, I'd stopped regressing to my stepdaughter's age, I'd illuminated old trauma, I'd chanted and Reikied and massaged and journaled and shamanic danced and natal charted and angel carded—why the hell couldn't I get a handle on real happiness??? Then one day, *A Course in Miracles,* a metaphysical text that channels the teachings of Christ, served me some truth about happiness in four words: **Forgive and be happy.**

Just forgiveness?

Yep, just forgiveness.

Most of us carry around a grudge of some sort, steadfastly believing that the offender is not worthy of our forgiveness because their behavior is beyond redemption. By maintaining this grudge, we grant this person power over us. As long as we stay hardened in aggression, bitterness, or fear, we do not have peace of mind. We surrender our happiness in exchange for grudge-y judgment.

Inside each of our heads is a brain that is in constant judgment mode. It's nothing to be ashamed of. At its best, judgment keeps us safe by guiding us to healthy choices. In its efforts to protect us, the brain also judges interpersonal relationships. When someone hurts us, it goes into hardcore protection mode. Defensiveness may manifest as offensiveness—anger, disappointment, or shock. In a mind that is unable to re-establish composure, forgiveness is inaccessible, and these reactions thicken into those aforementioned feelings of aggression, bitterness, or fear.

In a composed mind, these reactions will subside with forgiveness. Forgiveness washes through the brain with a conversation, with a physical release, with compassionate understanding, or with time. When we forgive someone who has hurt us, we free up space in our minds, we are relieved of the burden of judging another human, and we keep our personal power intact.

Let's take this construct into practice. Often, the person most harshly judged and least easily forgiven is yourself. I'm no exception, so I begin the forgiveness process by searching my mind for grudges I hold against myself: for eating 14 Newman's Own Ginger O's, for yelling at my kids, for being irresponsible with money, for not being born with green eyes (I always wanted green eyes), for gossiping, for wearing puff sleeves to prom, for crashing my truck, for serving breakfast for dinner, for watching *The Bachelorette*, for not doing anything about my tight hamstrings, for having a terrible singing voice… I bring it all to the surface, leaving nothing out.

Once I unearth a bunch of yuck, I zone in on one crappy thing at a time and observe my thoughts about each during a meditation sitting. It may look something like this:

Breathing in, I am happy. Breathing out, I invite Peace. Breathing in, I remember that fight with Michael when he told me I needed to take a deep breath. Breathing out, as if I don't know about deep breathing! I'm a committed meditator. I know about breathing. He always thinks he's right. His constant correcting makes me feel like I'm stupid. Maybe I am stupid. He's such an asshole. Wait, where was I? Breathing in, I'm getting really upset right now. Breathing out, my throat feels tight. Breathing in, my heart is pounding. Breathing out, this is so messed up! Breathing in, no wonder there's so much drama in my life! Breathing out, maybe I can get a prescription for Xanax. Breathing in, Xanax is a palindrome. Breathing out, like kayak and Hannah. Breathing in, my mind is wandering. Breathing out, I'm sitting on my couch meditating. Breathing in, I remember my breath. Breathing out, I breathe out. Breathing in, I breathe in. Breathing out, Michael is not really an asshole. (Sorry, Michael.) Breathing in, And I'm not stupid. Breathing out, I'm not stupid. Breathing in, I can forgive him, and I forgive myself. Breathing out, I'm okay.

Gnarly

Forgiving yourself sounds doable, right? Now what? Let's try forgiving something or someone really gnarly. This will likely require a longer sitting. Plant your tush on a cushion and choose your desired meditation approach (breath, music, candlelight, movement, etc.).

Next, state your forgiveness-based intention silently, then give yourself five to seven minutes to settle into your cushion or chair. The body will arrive first, perhaps the breath drops from the chest to the belly or your weight sinks a little deeper into your seat. You may hear your belly grumble or notice aches and pains creeping into your body. These are all normal parts of relaxation and awareness.

When the mind begins to wander, there are two choices available. You can: one, decide that the thoughts are brain clutter (i.e., my palindrome example), label them as such, forgive yourself, and return gently to breath or one-pointed awareness; or two, decide that the thoughts are worth exploring and let go of one-pointedness long enough to investigate with curiosity.

Label thoughts as they come up. *That's jealousy. That's panic. That's not true. That makes my heart hurt.* Always label with compassion. Even the most interesting thoughts begin to deteriorate into gibberish after a few minutes, so when you notice the mind repeating phrases like a scratched record that's skipping, trust that the thought's initial wisdom has imprinted on the brain and gently release the story, returning to breath.

If you are in a safe place physically and mentally, there may be opportunity for healing through insight. Go ahead and explore whatever appropriate thoughts come up. If the time isn't right to go deep, make a date with yourself to sit with those feelings in the near future. *I can't deal with you right now because I'm on my lunch break, and I have a presentation in 30 minutes. I promise that I will receive you, dear persistent and niggling thought, on Tuesday night before I go to bed.*

Tuesday night will most likely be uncomfortable. When you sit down on this hot date with yourself, try moving through your grudge or your stuck-ness by first dropping into your heart space. Proceed with something like this:

I'm aware that my thoughts, feelings, and sensations are created by my imagination and I thank you, God, for protecting my body from the stress produced by my chaotic mind. I forgive myself for these harmful, judgmental thoughts, specifically the ones about _____. This mental commotion has inspired me to seek peace. For this reason, I can be grateful for this internal drama, and I will use it as motivation to become my best self and pray for this person who distressed me. May I be peaceful and at ease. May _____ be peaceful and at ease. (Repeat the "may-I-may-you" lines of Metta over and over until you feel a shift in your heart space or in your mindset.)

When I practice forgiveness formally, I leave nothing and no one out. I forgive people for being mean to my kid, for stealing my fabulous Linda Farrow rose-tinted tea glasses, for not inviting me to that barbeque, for beating me at Monopoly, for being prettier than I am, for hitting me in the back of the head with a tennis ball… for everything.

In the fall of 2016, I spent a lot of time forgiving a particular presidential candidate. As the November election drew near, said candidate angered and confounded me more and more. During my forgiveness sessions, I'd shrink this human down to a tiny, helpless baby to diminish his massive ego. A crying orange infant with puckered face and floppy yellow hair made regular appearances in my Metta prayers as my challenging person. Wishing him peace helped me neutralize my disdain for him at the time. Little did I know I'd be rocking him in my arms and forgiving him for the next couple of years.

I worked this practice until I came to peace with our American-game-show-host-turned-President, accepting that his role in our third dimensional reality is to drag the nation's implicit memories up to the surface, kicking and screaming, so they can be healed in the light. This is a dirty job, one that I've had to do in a scaled down version in my own life. Everything worked out for the best with me, and I have faith that the same will happen for our beloved country.

If you decide that Metta forgiveness is a practice you'd like to engage, start with strangers. It's always easiest to forgive strangers. Forgive the telemarketer for pronouncing your name wrong. Forgive the DJ for playing Ariana Grande (again). Forgive the bus driver for stopping in a puddle and forgive the lady who took the last rotisserie chicken at the supermarket. In time, you'll become bolder and more skillful.

That said, you can't love everyone. Your humanness won't allow it. Forgiveness is an emotional and spiritual power tool that requires effort, and if you keep hanging out with weenies, you'll be swinging that tool so often you'll feel wiped out. Don't exhaust yourself trying to cast love and light on the people who drive you mad. Leave that to God. Leave that to Jesus. Leave that to Krishna and Mother Theresa and George Michael. Leave the challenging people in your life to those not in human form, because it's easier that way and also highly effective. Instead, focus on those whose mutual love you can trust.

Chapter Summary:
May I forgive and be happy. May you forgive and be happy. May we forgive and be happy.

Once you get really good at forgiving yourself and reconciling challenging interactions with others, you'll notice your life opening up in miraculous ways. Nothing will ever be perfect, but you'll see the perfection in everything. You will be ready to extend forgiveness to even the worst offenders.

Forgiveness is the key to your happiness, and it may be the most used practice in your mindfulness arsenal. Don't be selective about who you forgive. Let it rip—no matter how silly or small or how far in the past. If it pops into the mind, it's popping for a reason. Let your grievances be heard and forgiven. Trust that forgiveness is your primary purpose and compassionately relieve yourself of the burden of judgment.

Journal Prompts:
- Renew your commitment to forgiveness each day and pay attention to your thoughts in the days and weeks you practice. Record reconciliations in your journal.
- Do you catch yourself in petty irritation with particularly challenging friends, family members, or coworkers? Is it them or you? Is it hard to forgive them? Hard to forgive yourself?
- Are you surprised to notice how often atonement is required during the day? Does forgiveness feel liberating?
- One week after forgiving a person, revisit them in your mind. Do you feel different?

12

May I rise. May you rise. May we rise.

Wheeeeeeeee

There are some yucks that are harder to clean up than others. The abandonment grudge I'd been holding against Pop took root firmly in my early adolescence and caused me diverse suffering over many years. Back in high school, I considered myself truly unlovable, unworthy of goodness. I was jealous. I was distrustful. I turned in half-ass assignments at school. I binge ate. I starved myself. I lied. I fought with my sister. I obsessed over boys who treated me like garbage.

Strangely, at the time I had no idea why my adolescence was so messy. We didn't talk about things like abandonment in my family. Forgiveness was not presented as a healing option. I never saw a social worker or sat down with the school psychologist. It was more like, *Well, this is it. Let's keep on living.* And we somehow managed—or rather mismanaged.

Through many adult years of psychotherapy and painfully honest self-work, countless scribbly journals and my own rocky marriage, I eventually forgave Pop for skipping out on his fatherly duties and accepted that he walked a path that led him far away from home. He wasn't a bad person. His intention was not to blow up my teen years. He just couldn't do any better. I never made excuses for him. I plainly accepted that this man was fighting an inner battle that had very little to do with me. I didn't need to shoulder his struggles anymore. A not-so-tiny forgiveness shift occurred in 2009, but we have to time travel down a wormhole to get the whole story. Let's go! *Wheeeeeeeee!*

Back in the 1970s and '80s, Pop's dreams were always much bigger than the reality his small suburban family could provide. He worked tirelessly to develop a bilingual education program at Boston English High School. He spoke passionately about the growing Latino movement in Boston and was repeatedly invited by Harvard University to lecture about his work. He was even invited to earn a Master's in Education on full scholarship. I attended one of his lectures once and distinctly remember standing behind him while a mob of Ivy League co-eds rushed the lectern after he spoke, eager to ask questions and share their own anecdotes. His students loved him, his peers respected him, and his family thought he was nuts.

Pop walked down the street pinching a joint in one hand and flashing a peace sign in the other. His signature look was a "No Nukes" sweatshirt, overalls, and long curly hair wrapped up in a red bandanna.

No apologies.

As an adult, I appreciate his unwillingness to conform, but as a kid, I found him absolutely ridiculous. He spent too many of his days off high as a kite, weekends playing guitar in my grandmother's living room, and afternoons slumbering on the family room couch, maybe cracking open his eyes to watch *The Gong Show*. Either the man had a thing for Chuck Barris, or he was depressed before we became a Prozac nation.

On December 27, 1986, he could no longer hold space for work, family, dreams, and the demons in his head, so he left us.

It was sad.

May I rise. May you rise. May we rise.

Magic

But there was a light—a bright light—in my story of fatherless daughterhood. It sparked in 2001 when Michael introduced me to Mother Caroline Academy and Education Center, a tuition-free middle school in Dorchester for bright girls of limited financial means. He'd been involved with the school's fundraising mission for years and brought me to their annual spring event in Jamaica Plain where we were greeted by dozens of smiling girls in plaid kilts, knee socks, and oversized red blazers, all singing, chattering, laughing, and jumping Double Dutch. Suddenly a nun came out of nowhere and hopped between the ropes. She was really good. A couple of other nuns ran in and did the same. These people were brimming with joy, and they made me laugh out loud. A love affair with Mother Caroline began.

For several years I volunteered for the Academy's development office, but I began to yearn for a personal connection with the students. In 2009, I signed up to mentor a child. After navigating several awkward tweenage meet-and-greets, I introduced myself to a charming 13-year-old girl named Leidi.

Leidi and I chatted easily. She was an old soul, thoughtful, inquisitive, interesting, genuine, beautiful, and daddy-less like me. Water seeks its own level and our bond was instantaneous.

Years later, while road-tripping one Sunday afternoon, I mentioned to Leidi that my father taught bilingual students at Boston English. She said that her mom went to Boston English. Some quick math led us to realize that our parents were there at the same time. And since Leidi's mom was Puerto Rican, the likelihood of her knowing Pop was good. Really good. Really, really good.

Leidi called that night. Her mom had class with my father. He was her mentor.

I hung up the phone and digested the news. My long-lost deadbeat father was my mentee's mother's mentor. I burst into tears. Fat tears. A full-on contorted-face-heaving-chest ugly cry.

I cried because for the first time in 27 years, I felt grateful for this crazy hippie I called Pop. I cried because the world is small, and the Universe is complex. I cried for another tiny shift: no matter how far I ran from my father, the elasticity of our shared, unresolved suffering would snap back on me and force us to collide again and again in unexpected, sometimes beautiful ways.

In a flash of clarity, I saw the parallels between our unique purposes, our mutual desire to make the world a better place, and the genetic gifts he passed to me that have allowed me to live a life of my own choosing, just as he did. I understood in that moment that my life was built for miracles, full of synchronicity and magic.

There were no coincidences.

Leidi was my karmic gift, one I was so happy to accept.

The shift involving Leidi eliminated longstanding bitterness, leaving me lighter, less burdened, almost sparkly. Because I had adopted the energy of forgiveness—in other words, made forgiveness a priority—the Universe supported me by providing experiences that could help me transmute any remaining suffering associated with grudge holding, which I knew would open a portal to happiness.

Forgiveness became my superpower.

Discernment

There was still some residual yuck, though. I could feel it sitting between my happiness and me. I went on a meditation retreat in 2014 to spend a whole week focused on complete and total transmutation of manifestations involving implicit memories of abandonment and rejection. About three days into the retreat, surrounded by 250 fellow meditators, I dissolved into tears when I realized I'd been unconsciously aligning myself with people who made me feel the way Pop made me feel—small. When I surveyed my inner circle of friends and family from a place of compassionate neutrality, I became aware of interpersonal mismatches that resulted in friction, and this friction consumed mental energy that blocked me from engaging happier thoughts.

Relationships are soul contracts that last only as long as they serve all parties. Sometimes they expire naturally. Other times, we hold onto relationships longer than we should, out of fear or habit, obligation or a sense of safety. Like pretty much everything else in life, relationships are fluid and ever-changing. It's necessary to edit, renegotiate, or even void agreements that we make at one point in time to reflect what's happening at another point in time.

We grow and change a little every day. Sometimes relationships keep pace, sometimes they don't. It's not personal. It just is. After a long, quiet week of navel gazing, I recognized this and knew I needed to create distance between the people in my life who were not a match for my current personal vibration. Discerning action was required.

Little by little, either through direct, uncomfortable conversations or through slowly lessening time spent with particular people, I worked to curate a smaller, safer social and family circle for myself: one in which I felt wholly loved, respected, and supported. This was not done to exclude or blame, it was done to protect my heart and mind from continuous exposure to chaos, competition, and confusion.

I meditated on each of these relationships, offered gratitude for the life lessons my loved ones offered me, provided and asked forgiveness for any pain caused, and thanked all higher selves involved for rewriting contracts or allowing them to expire peacefully.

If you are white knuckling relationships with people who do not match your vibration, then you are exposing yourself to misunderstanding and potentially to judgment. Judgment and happiness do not coexist well, so you must give one up. They each require effort; you have to decide which one is more worthy of your headspace.

Ascension

In mid-September of 2017, Pop died of natural causes in San Juan, Puerto Rico, hours before Hurricane Maria ripped through the island. He was 69 and alone. Wild weather and government bureaucracy slowed the notification process, so it was many months before we learned he'd passed.

Exactly a week after his death, Penelope and I flew to Lima, Peru for a mother-daughter adventure. We celebrated her 13th birthday with a shamanic retreat to Peru's Sacred Valley led by my mind-blowingly talented friends Pierre Gerraud and Janice Johnson. While in Macchu Pichu, our group of nine travelers prepared for a ritual by hiking along the Urubamba River, collecting stones that represented people we wanted to forgive.

This was my chance to release Pop once and for all.

I chose the heaviest stones I could carry. We reached a wooden bridge surrounded by dense jungle where, one at a time, we tossed the weights into the water.

I watched Pop and his yuck sink.

I felt free.

We continued on, hiking to a sacred waterfall. The water was so cold it hurt to touch, but in order to maximize the experience, we were instructed to dunk so that our entire bodies and hair were completely soaked. With a lot of yelping and whooping, we submerged then scrambled downriver to some rocks where we sat and let the powerful, frigid flow rush into us. After ten minutes or so of giggles through chattering teeth, we dried off and shivered our way back to the riverbank where we each received a multidimensional shamanic healing on an ancient stone altar. After watching several women undergo dramatic, physical soul work, I stepped up to take my turn, and guess what happened? I laid down on that hard, old slab of granite and belly laughed. I laughed so hard my body shook and salty rivers poured from my eyes. I tried to hold it back because the ceremony was sacred, and laughter seemed inappropriate.

But the giggles would not, could not be contained.

My happiness rose.

I risked looking weird and howled. As Pierre and Janice worked on me, they started laughing, too. Because my eyes were closed, I couldn't see that my giggles were spilling onto the crowd of spiritual seekers standing around us, resulting in curled lips and toothy smiles. As grudge and yuck released, the essence of happiness remained.

I was emotionally ascending.

The experience taught me that healing can happen in a thousand ways. Laughter works just as well as tears. We can evolve through pain and suffering, just as we can evolve through happiness and health. It also taught me that my energy touches other people. I can drain onlookers with the density of my resistance, or I can inspire them by allowing my authenticity to flow through. Like I said before, both are okay, but the latter is much more fun.

Chapter Summary:

May I rise. May you rise. May we rise.

Healing can be as windy and unpredictable as a river. You just never know how it will come through. I hope that this chapter relays a few ideas for you: 1) taking on the energy of healing opens doors to experiences that heal; 3) every experience you live through consciously leads you closer to Love; 3) by bravely practicing discernment, you distance yourself from suffering and spare yourself the need to heal yourself again in the future; 4) **expect miracles, not outcomes.**

Journal Prompts:

- Is there anyone you *think* you've forgiven, but you really haven't forgiven *all the way*? Who is it? How do they show up for you in day to day life?
- Search your mind for powerful real-life characters from your childhood. Who lifted you up? Who weighed you down? Do their opinions of you still inform the person you are today? In beneficial or detrimental ways?
- Who currently in your life feels like sunshine? Go ahead and list the people. Who feels like a thundercloud? Call them out, too. Are you willing to make some changes to your inner circle?

13

May I live in alignment. May you live in alignment. May we live in alignment.

Light

There is a path that serves the greatest good, a path that can release you from ancestral karma and bring peace to future generations. That path begins with you.

Stepping into it is revelatory. It's as if there's been a shaft of light beaming next to you your whole life. All along you've been remotely aware of its presence but afraid to step into it.

Perhaps by accident, one day your finger passes through the light. You get a little shock. It's exciting. It feels surprisingly awesome. You play with it. Tentatively, you allow your shoulder to pass through, but pull out quickly because you've never seen yourself that way, and it's sort of scary. The light feels simultaneously familiar and fascinating.

In time, you get used to flirting with the light, and you test out some other body parts. Your toes, your belly, your kneecaps. Occasionally you dip bravely and completely into the shaft, but it's hard to stay there for very long because feeling healthy can be uncomfortable, or because you are so well practiced at hiding in the dark.

The more time you spend standing in that shaft of light, though, the more natural you feel in it. The darkness begins to feel like a dream. Try dropping into meditation right in the center of this beam. Your entire body is illuminated, divine. You may feel a glow in your heart space, a feeling of comfort, joy, safety, or hope. Cultivate it, welcome it, fuse it with your authenticity.

We can live in the light all the time, and teach our children to do the same, but we have to be willing to shed some sticky, dense layers of karma first. This is a deliberate process that requires three wholesome actions: release, reflection, and reinvention. These steps will not only welcome awesome synchronicities, but they'll also help us create space for uplifting experiences and new opportunities. That amazing thing we're waiting for is not going to appear until we ditch some old yuck. We need to prove that our mind is strong enough to handle it first.

This process of releasing, reflecting, and reinventing will look different for you than it does for me. But I can walk you through a few of my own discarded layers to give you some ideas on how to further awaken, align, and plant your ass firmly in the light. Let's check this process out together.

Release

The first major release for me was breaking up with booze. I know. Jesus drank wine. I know. *I know!* I'm not so sure whether his wine drinking was about taking the edge off a long day or about the lack of clean water, but regardless, he drank it. My own release of alcohol is not a judgment on your ritualistic Friday night cocktail or your date night glass of Montepulciano. I'm just sharing my personal experience, which is this: throwing up on my own legs to keep from making a mess on the floor; narrowly escaping *God-knows-what* after guzzling a glass of roofied wine at The White House Correspondents Dinner (of all places); vomiting the previous night's watermelon cosmos into a plastic bag while my soon-to-be stepdaughter watched sympathetically; blacking out after no less than 40 incidences of binge drinking.

Alcohol makes me feel out of control. It is a depressant that results in puke, regrets, and bed spins. Booze is in direct opposition to my body, mind, and spirit. So aside from an occasional tequila, I don't drink it anymore.

There is another thing about alcohol that is pretty uncool: drunk moms. Those late afternoon playgroups when we all arrive toting toddlers and bottles of pinot?

Let's talk about it.

If you could stop hating this idea (and perhaps me) for a moment, you might be willing to agree that slogging back white wine spritzers while our kids play with Tinker Toys is not our finest parenting choice—if not for the impracticality of pumping and dumping or driving kids home slightly buzzed, then maybe for the fact that kids don't enjoy our sloppy kisses, uncomfortably loud laughter, or unpredictable behavior.

I still remember my Great Uncle Neil sliming my five-year-old mouth with his tangy-boozy-slobber-smooches at the St. Patrick's Day parade in Southie every year. My fellow Irish Bostonians will surely commiserate: the third Sunday in March is forever synonymous with the squeal of green plastic trumpets on Broadway, embroidered shamrock stickers that left white goo on our winter coats, and drunk relatives draped in lawn chairs on the sidewalk, lip kissing everyone who passed by. For me, that day is forever associated with whiskey breath and feeling small.

My point is, don't think your drinking goes unnoticed by your babies.

This is a sensitive, personal topic about which drinkers may quickly become defensive and feel judged. Talking about another person's alcohol consumption is like touching their open wound;

they naturally recoil when anyone tries to peel the bandage back and poke at what's going on underneath. But it must be done because, as Rumi said, "The wound is the place the light enters." We'll pick this back up with journal prompts in the chapter summary. You can't wait, right?

Release can be hard for us humans because, for better or worse, we absolutely love our habits. Unfortunately, a lot of our habits do not serve our highest purpose, so it's important to assess some of these sticklers from a neutral vantage, then decide if we're engaging in routines and activities that support our alignment or distract us from it.

Pinpointing bad habits will likely take minimal effort. We know the dumb things we do. But let's get on the same page here. Bad habits are different from full-blown addictions. Chronic complaining and abusing Oxy are two different animals. One can likely be settled through awareness and the other requires rehab and counseling.

Once we decide which habits are the most debilitating, we can make a plan to release them. We start this process by gently rearranging our schedules and environments, so that we are not constantly tempted into trouble.

Is your book club full of catty ladies? Drop it. Is your closet full of clothes you don't wear? Purge it. Does your job make your blood pressure skyrocket? Quit it. Is Facebook occupying four hours of your day? Fuck it. You can do these things. You are allowed. In fact, you are more than allowed. You are urged. This is Your One Sacred Life and you must honor it by exposing yourself to the light.

Reflect

For me, it was necessary to release my alcohol intake completely, and there was a major void with the commitment. From having to say, "No, I'm not pregnant," a dozen times to physically not holding a glass in my hand at cocktail parties, there was a clear shift in my party girl role that needed to be acknowledged mindfully.

I started staying home more. When I did venture out to barbeques and boozy social gatherings, I would often feel like a child at the adult table. Other times I'd worry that my abstinence implied that I was a recovering addict. A friend once called me a loser for not drinking. Michael regularly and publicly called me a teetotaler, which not only made me feel self-conscious, but also self-righteous.

At first, I got mad, but the anger moved through naturally. I replaced those labels and feelings with other labels and feelings that felt truer, like *nonconformist* and *sovereign, strong* and *self-knowing*. I observed the shift with mindfulness.

I refilled some of the party-time emptiness with television (not so great), and the rest with my kids (so great). I got curious about the feeling of *not* going with the social flow. I checked in with my emotions, my thoughts, my body, and I watched patiently (for years) until the feeling eventually passed.

The hours and energy that you once put into bad habits leave a void; spending unoccupied time in that void can make you feel lost. Engaging mindful reflection in that void can also be difficult because it's uncomfortable, and most people hate to feel uncomfortable.

Try anyway.

There will likely be sensations inside your body that make you feel anxious. There may be people or places that you miss visiting… Most of all, there will be large swaths of time that are now free and clear to do…. *Ugh. I don't know. What do I do?*

The reflection process may burn with a bit of depression or anxiety. These empty feelings may smolder and smoke for a few days or weeks, making your world look a little fuzzy. Try to be gentle with yourself and stay true to the space you've created. In his book *Tantra, The Supreme Understanding*, tantric master Osho writes, "If you stop [this activity] you will start something else—because the disease doesn't change by changing the symptoms." Rather than fill the void with another distraction or activity—like organizing your digital photo library or adopting a rescue puppy (I've done both)—just sit with the void. *Huh. So this is what release feels like. This is emptiness.* During this time, it is possible to hold that space open for the inspired, light-filled layers that *do* serve your highest purpose.

Patience is an absolute must, as is trust.

There will be times when you sit down to hold that space and search your mind for help from Jesus or Buddha or Krishna or angels or dead grandparents and all you hear is crickets. In the silence, you may feel abandoned by God. You'll feel alone. Please turn on The Beatles. Seriously. The Beatles. Listen to *Let it Be* or my favorite song of all time, *Hey Jude*, "Take a sad song and make it better." I've lately discovered the wicked awesome joy of dancing in my kitchen to Queen's *Don't Stop Me Now*. It's like a direct line to heaven. Music reminds us that we're not alone and inspires us to live above our circumstances.

Reinvent

Eventually, the day came that I could say "yes" to events that felt good to me, that I could toast with my water glass and focus on the blessings and the friends and the smiles and the love, not the insecurity. (Though if I'm toasting with my friend Christianne, she will still force me to drink from her glass of wine because toasting with a glass of water ensures seven years of bad sex, something a newly single lady cannot risk.) My abstinence practice is not perfect, but I'm happy with it. In the last 15 years I've had alcohol no more than a dozen times. A few of those times, I've allowed myself to get silly drunk, just for fun.

In the name of fun, I reinvented my weekends, registering for spiritual retreats, picking up yoga, getting certified in multiple energy healing modalities, and learning how to do Numerology and read Tarot. Many of the people I met at these events matched my emotional or spiritual vibration. Our conversations stimulated and expanded my mind. We laughed and danced and healed... and the strongest drink we shared was green tea.

I'm still a party girl at heart—social, curious, experimental; and I love to love people. So, a couple of years ago I decided to redirect some of my old booze-bag energy toward the Buddhist practice *Tantra,* which, like most people, I thought was purely about having amazing sex. Orgasms sounded like a fun time to me.

I skipped visiting the library for books this time and ordered a dozen paperbacks on Tantra and sex from Amazon. I needed more instruction and scanned the web for classes. While it's not tantric per se, OMGYES.com is a membership site that features a series of interviews with women of all ages and races who look like people you'd see in your neighborhood. They demonstrate on camera exactly how they reach orgasm. The exact opposite of porn, OMGYES.com is educational and supportive and beautiful.

Now there are more courses popping up that are specifically devoted to Tantra, but at the time only a few existed. One was an Udemy course posted by a 20-something woman named Adelka Skotak. For much of it, Adelka sits in the grass in her back yard and chatters on about nurturing a loving relationship with yourself. After the amount of self-work I'd done over the years, I found myself feeling antsy while waiting for this sex guru to get to the big "how-to," but I'm so glad I didn't click fast-forward on her, because she told a funny little story that stayed with me. In summary, she went to a party one night and suddenly decided that she didn't want to be there, so she left. Her sage tantric advice, delivered in a sexy Eastern European accent, went something like, "If you don't want to be at the party, just leave the party."

Ding!

Words to live by.

The bigger message is: know yourself; love yourself. Respect yourself. If you're doing something that makes you feel bad or doesn't sit in that shaft of light called *your divine vibration*, recognize it. Honor it. Don't apologize. Just leave the party, then do the thing that you really want to do.

I still love Tantra, and not just because I've learned to have head-spinning orgasms. In Tantra, every part of ourselves must be seen and accepted in the light. It's a philosophy without secrets. Its practices encourage total self-love in our physical form. Physical mastery is a great portal to consciousness. And it's *fun!* We deserve pleasure. Pleasure is a reflection of self-love.

Nothing exists that is not Love.

Chapter Summary:

> *May I live in alignment. May you live in alignment.*
> *May we live in alignment.*

After doing all this work releasing, reflecting, and reinventing, my advice to others is this: welcome honest conversations with yourself about the things in your life that no longer serve you, and affirm that your reinvention is always toward wholesomeness and positivity. Own your experiences. Don't let experiences own you or turn you into someone you're not; don't compromise your position in the light in exchange for low-vibrational behavior; but don't be limited by personal dogma either. Life is fluid, always changing. One day you are this way, another day you are that way. **All ways are acceptable ways… it's just that some hurt, and some don't.** This shift can happen with effort or with time, whichever is required. But it always happens when you are truly ready to align.

Journal Prompts:

- Everything we do, we do for a reason. Think about something you'd benefit from releasing. Why do you turn to it regularly? What's the appeal? What void does it fill?
- Conjure up your earliest memories surrounding alcohol and reflect on your feelings. Or perhaps your kids already have some of their own they'd be willing to share. Write it all down.
- *A Course in Miracles* says, "Your purpose is to see the world through your own holiness. Thus are you and the world blessed together." Take a moment to reflect and write. How do you hold holiness within your vibration? Are you ready to be all the light that you are? Are you waiting to become lighter? Do you believe the world waits with you?
- When was the last time you had an orgasm? Not the last time you came, but had a *real* orgasm? How does your answer make you feel? Is physical mastery something you're interested in? Are you worthy of physical pleasure? Why or why not?

14

May I let go. May you let go. May we let go.

Heavy

Several years ago, I hosted a Saturday morning yard sale; my front lawn was a graveyard for misfit decor, obsolete electronics, outgrown toys, and battered sports equipment. I watched with relief as old treasures were released from purgatory by folks who promised to breathe life back into them.

We often talk about lightening our heavy loads in an emotional way, but there's no need for metaphor when physically disencumbering 1,500 pounds of impulse buys from the basement. The purge is deeply connected to an emotional unraveling that is both healing and heartbreaking.

I confess I struggled with the purge. I specifically struggled with several large Rubbermaid bins full of clothing samples, ghosts of my profession past. I am a serial small business owner and spent most of my 20s and 30s birthing creative enterprises that fizzled and died before maturity. (It's hard to be a winner when you believe with all your heart that you're a loser.) My boldest endeavor was a golf apparel line for women and children called Van Linsey. It was three years old and doing well, sold in 13 country clubs and receiving great press.

Just before I was to deliver the 2009 spring collection, I birthed Xavier. This child was all love and wisdom from the start, filled with soulful newborn knowing. He helped me understand that manufacturing clothes (or anything) was not in alignment with my spirit.

I finished the season, packed up my trade show booth, fell out of touch with customers, and watched from the nursing rocker as a thick layer of dust settled on my sewing machine.

Though at the time of the yard sale, the golf line had been resting six feet under for many years, I still felt pangs of guilt, shame, and regret for burying it alive. Each time I'd glimpse those bins stacked in the closet, I'd immediately start ruminating on the money I'd wasted, the way others must have judged me for folding my business, and of course the success I could've been. I felt stuck, unable to go forward or backward, in a purgatory of my own.

Those Rubbermaid bins were like tombs, haunted by sample-sized specters who rattled chains made of exposed zippers and ruffled collars. Those phantoms held me back, quietly murmuring, "You never finish anything, Vanessa. Good ideas. No follow through. Why bother starting anything new when you're born to fail? You're discardable, unworthy, a reject; your father was right. Remember that!"

They whispered mean things to me, but I kept them anyway. Maybe you've held onto your whispery shadows, too—there's something beautifully painful about suffering, about knowing we're inadequate.

Our shortcomings and insufficiencies are ghost stories we know so well. We can recite every line by heart. And we are strangely comfortable with them. If our dark tales weren't here, if our lack and our suffering weren't holding us back, we'd have to step fully into that bright loving light that forces us to live fully. Living fully can be scary. There's risk in the fullness. *What if we fail? What if we disappoint?*

But the scariest thing for me is always this: *What if I succeed? Do I deserve success? If I deserve success, does that mean I'm good? Can I accept that I am good? Am I even worthy?*

Oh, my God.

Am I worthy?

On September 20, 2014, I stared down those Rubbermaid bins stacked neatly on my porch. I delivered my best Clint Eastwood squint and threatened, "It's you or me."

And I chose me.

I forgave myself for giving up on the business, for letting a pastel-hued dream fade to black, for not shouldering those clothes to the mountaintop of golf apparel, for choosing motherhood *singularly*, and I courageously dragged the bins onto the lawn, displaying them neatly… behind a large holly bush. (Maybe I was only half ready to let them go.)

Space

Two hours into the sale, an old lady wandered behind the bushes and pointed a finger at my plastic mausoleum of sportswear, "I'll give you $10 for everything in this box."

"*Pssshht,* 10 dollars?" I snorted. "You could start a whole business with what's in that box. There's thousands of dollars' worth of retail merchandise in that b—"

The lady looked at me in a way that I can only describe as neutral.

I shut my eyes and took a deep breath, "Okay, it's yours for 20."

"I'm not buying it for me," said the old lady in a thick Caribbean accent. "I'm bringing it to Haiti for mission."

I suddenly had a visual of a gorgeous Haitian woman walking slowly down a bustling city street, wearing my light, breathable resort wear, looking crisp and cool in the hot, hot sun. I hauled forward every bin I had, transferred their contents into huge white Glad bags, and recruited a friend to carry my Supima cotton treasures into the old lady's station wagon. I hugged her 35 times, then accepted her 10 bucks gratefully.

My face contorted from smiles to sobs, back to smiles then more sobs.

The beauty of the story was that by clearing out my physical space, I was able to create the emotional space needed to experience full-presence parenting. It also opened a door for the creativity I'd need down the line for new endeavors. I felt lighter, less burdened, braver.

Lighter

I cannot say enough about the emotional and physical strain our material possessions have on us. C. JoyBell C. writes, "You will find that it is necessary to let things go; simply for the reason that they are heavy. So let them go, let go of them. I tie no weights to my ankles." The catharsis I experienced by physically releasing my golf apparel line was the first time I understood the weighted burden of holding onto ideas and possessions that no longer serve me. I remember cleaning up the front lawn that afternoon and staring up at my luxe, oversized house, wondering if there was more that I could release.

For years, I'd been hearing patient whispers from deep inside my heart, urging me to sell our home. The ignored murmurs manifested in my low back, making my muscles chronically squeeze and ache, a lot like the IBS but less embarrassing.

The house was gorgeous, renovated to our taste, and perfect walking distance to school, town, and train. Architected for the world's best games of hide-n-seek, it served magically for parties and playdates. It inspired creativity and safety and healing. We infinitely adored our neighbors. And there was another reason to keep the house: I knew I would not be able to create a new home as Michael's wife, and the thought of disrupting our family paralyzed me. For those reasons and more, Michael and I both tuned out the quiet urges to sell.

Eventually, though, the whispers turned to screams. Caring for all that square footage while mothering a brood of kids overwhelmed me—especially so when I decided to open another new business. Selling started to make logical sense as Michael and I inched closer to splitting up. In October 2015, we put the house on the market. The day we signed with our broker, my chronic back pain lifted. I haven't felt it since.

I'm convinced that if I had been patient enough to sit down and meditate with that pain at length, I would've made the connection much sooner and spared myself five years of back maintenance by way of acupuncture, Reiki, chiropractic, and a dozen other holistic healing modalities. But had I not experienced the pain, I would not have aggressively sought all those healing modalities and would have missed out on the amazing learning and growth that came from it. We can evolve through pain or we can evolve through joy. It's all good, but one is a lot more fun.

Chapter Summary:
May I let go. May you let go. May we let go.

To the world, seekers like us look healthy, unruffled, maybe even serene. One may conjure images of Gautama Buddha sitting under the bodhi tree, with his *Mona Lisa* smile and his creaseless forehead. We meditators know better. We know that the Buddha was fighting for his life. His inner landscape was likely chaotic as he battled

Mara's armies for three excruciating years, eventually finding nirvana through stillness and vigilance. This process of awakening is not easy. Sometimes the battle takes place in your head and sometimes in your front yard. Do whatever it takes to release excess, as this is an important step in cultivating happiness. **God wants us to be happy.** It's that simple. Shuddering off the weights we've accumulated and rising in joy is like a fast track to ascension. Our spirit grows stronger and vibrates faster when we release ourselves of burdens.

Journal Prompts:
- When was the last time you had a big physical purge? Are you comfortable reassigning your old stuff? Are you attached to anything that's burdensome to own?
- Are there weights around your ankles? Do you know what they are? Are you willing to shed the weights and release the pain? Or do you use the pain as an excuse to hold you back? Can you use the pain to gain valuable new insights?
- Would you rather rise in joy? Are you worthy of joy?
- If you knew that letting go of something would result in a happier life, would you do it? Would it feel like a threat to your safety? To your conditioning? To other people's expectations or standards of happiness?

Intermission

May I take you aside for a moment and talk mother-to-mother, seeker-to-seeker? If you have experienced awakening, you'll understand how powerful it is. If you have experienced awakening as a parent while living with your children, you will understand what a blasted tease it is. It's as if you are ready to soar with the angels and shout from the rooftops, but your car just broke down, the fridge is empty, and your kids are squabbling fervently over who's the better flute player. No one cares that you're an evolved human being. Your kids just want you to take them places, make them food, and judge their woodwind face-offs. My sister-love bestie Alexis put it this way, "Mothering is an experience that requires us to be incredibly terrestrial."

While there are times when you can rise above it all and remain the badass, newly attuned, high-vibing mamacita you are, there are other times when you can't help but get sucked back into density by your kids and their daily dramas.

Happiness is a choice that requires great courage. Be brave, momma, be brave.

Part 2

THEN YOUR
FAMILY

15

May I be protected. May you be protected. May we be protected.

Hard

Mindfulness-based practices inspire us to uncover, understand, and undo our own unhealthy habitual behavior: recalibrating the emotional trajectory of our families not toward human perfectionism, but toward conscious Perfection.

If the idea sounds lofty, or even unattainable, let me swear something to you. I spent my first 30 years sky high on the yuck: insecurity, jealousy, depression, and volatility. Spiritually based mental health has been and continues to be like ongoing rehab for me, reminding me that **I am not the bullshit. I am the light.**

I know this works. I know that mindfulness makes peace possible because I engage it every single day, and even on the days when anything that possibly can go wrong does, I recover into peace.

This does not mean that I am free of suffering. This does not mean I will forever feel empowered and composed. This does not mean I'm a perfect person, a perfect business partner, a perfect friend, a perfect sister, and certainly not a perfect mother.

I have screamed at my kids. I have spanked them, called them jerks, swatted blindly at their kneecaps from the driver's seat of a minivan, made impulse purchases to placate them, and held their bedroom doors shut while they howled in dissent from the other side. I have let them watch age-inappropriate movies, ignored them while they fought, hidden in the closet devouring their Halloween candy, looked at my iPhone while they told me about *blah-blah-blah*, and forgotten to pick them up after practice. I've done these things like a cool cucumber. I've done these things like Joan Crawford in *Mommie Dearest*.

Fortunately for my children, and most of all for myself, since committing to a mindfulness practice, any screaming, squeezing, or swearing I do is not only less frequent, but it is also done with full awareness.

Case in point: a couple of years ago, I remember peeling my six-year-old's vice grip from the banister as I dragged his thrashing body upstairs to his room. Xavier had just smashed his sister's vulva with a lacrosse stick. His arms flailed wildly, tearing framed snapshots of smiling children off the wall as we ascended. (The irony was not lost on me.) I broke a sweat hauling him to time out, my back one twisty kick away from a trip to the chiropractor. While this humbling family moment unraveled, my mindfulness practice engaged. My thoughts looked something like this:

My arms are manhandling Xavier, muscles working. My jaw bites down hard on anger, the wrinkles between my eyes deepening with each screechy protest. I observe. My shoulders hoist to my earlobes as my coil constricts around Xavier's waist. I want to pinch him on purpose. I resist on purpose. I hear my own little voice wonder if we should've stopped at three kids. And then, a whisper of compassion: It won't always be this way. A pause. Deep breath in. Long breath out. More screaming. This child is hurting, and he needs love. Another deep breath in. One long exhale into my vice grip. I watch myself putting the boy down, regaining composure, forgiving myself for being totally exasperated and

127

totally normal.

This is deep-seated composure. This is mindful parenting. And don't let your seemingly-perfect-yogi-friend-who-grows-all-her-own-food-and-looks-like-she-showers-everyday convince you that mindful parenting is sitting on a cushion surrounded by your mala-beaded children, meditating on world peace and chanting *Om Mani Padme Hum*. Mindful parenting—and specifically mindful discipline—is hard. It's full-on. It's humbling. It's raw. It's lonely. It has nothing to do with them and everything to do with you. *Sing it, Dalai Lama. First you, then your family.*

Composure is a balanced way of being. When we are composed, we are relaxed, ready, and receptive. We are at peace. Buddhists call this equanimity. An ideal emotional condition for good mental health, composure is a gift we give to ourselves, and to the planet. Imagine a world in which people felt deeply at peace and interacted with each other from a place of composure, compassion, and sanity.

Actually, forget the world for a minute. Just imagine a whole day where your children choose to operate from composure. Go ahead and picture it: a new day begins as your happy children bound into the kitchen, smiling with recently brushed teeth. Their hair is combed, their homework is complete, their feet are wrapped in clean socks. Your oldest observes compassionately and silently that, once again, you didn't have time to hit the grocery store and subsequently breakfast is slim pickings. She calmly announces, "Little bro, there's only one cinnamon chip muffin left, and I know you really want it. Instead of me scarfing it while you freak out like usual, how 'bout we split it? That way we'll avoid a big fight and we might even get to school on time." He agrees and they share breakfast peacefully before leaving.

Thief

Okay, time to wake up. In the real world, our kids live full throttle, manipulating the world and the people around them in ways that enthrall us and infuriate us, awe us and terrify us, thrill us and shame us. Their drama, drama, drama leaves us longing for the capable, uncomplicated steadiness of... well, nothing in this world is uncomplicated or steady, but a little slice of sanity would be nice.

A Course in Miracles says, "There are no small upsets. They are all equally disturbing to [your] peace of mind." In other words, anticipating the fallout as you watch your child devour the last, coveted cinnamon chip muffin has the same physiological effect as finding out your spouse has gambled away the family's nest egg. It doesn't seem like the two should bear equal weight, but they do. Want to meet the resident composure thief?

Say hello to cortisol. Cortisol is a hormone secreted by your adrenal glands, two triangular-shaped organs that live just above your kidneys. At the risk of oversimplification, cortisol is the reason you are here today. If not for this quick-acting hormone, your primitive ancestors would have been gobbled up by tigers thousands of years ago.

Cortisol, also known as "the stress hormone," shuts down non-essential bodily functions and provides the body with everything it needs to fight, flee, or freeze. Cortisol overrides your immune and reproductive systems (you're not worried about healing a cut or making babies when you're about to be someone's lunch) and temporarily disables bone and muscle growth (no wonder I was so fucking short as a kid). It increases gastric acid production in the belly and stimulates sebum oil production in the skin (maybe if you taste really disgusting, you'll turn off that predator). Cortisol raises blood sugar and insulin levels for a big burst of energy. It sends lactic acid to your muscles so you can pump those arms and legs, and it expands your lung capacity so you can oxygenate your body and run top speed. All of this and more happens in a blink, without any conscious effort. Pretty amazing, right?

Cortisol is designed to hang out in your body for short stints. If you walked around jacked up on cortisol all day long, you'd look and feel absolutely INSANE. Can you imagine feeling stressed all the time? Feeling like you're always running away from something or chasing something or hiding from something?

Hmmmm... Come to think of it, this is exactly how your life may look some days. Traffic, money, terrorists, deadlines, relationships, work, sordid pasts, kids, over-scheduling, *Goddammit, why didn't I buy more cinnamon chip muffins??!!!* All of these situations stimulate cortisol production. And those are just the obvious stress triggers. Surely your life is dappled with complexities that people couldn't even imagine. If this describes you, cortisol may overproduce in your body a dozen times a day or more. This is not good. Here are four powerful reasons why:

1. When cortisol floods your hippocampus (the part of your brain responsible for memory and emotional responses), it kills brain cells. Fortunately, the hippocampus protects itself with something called brain-derived neurotrophic factor or BDNF. Unfortunately, when cortisol secretes chronically, BDNF cannot keep up with the demand and your brain cells bite it.

2. Cortisol thins the skin by depleting it of hyaluronic acid, a moisture retainer, stripping it of elasticity and suppleness. Additionally, it triggers inflammation resulting in damaged skin cells. The stress hormone also produces more sebum in your skin. Sebum is an oily substance that mixes with your

dead skin cells and clogs up hair follicles. Clogged follicles lead to... you guessed it. Acne, pimples, cysts. Ugh.

3. Cortisol interrupts the production of serotonin, the neurotransmitter that relays messages in the brain, including messages about mood, sex, and appetite, among other things. Serotonin is called the "feel good hormone," and an imbalance may severely influence your mood and drop you into depression.

4. One in ten people experience the discomfort of a peptic ulcer. While ulcers are believed to be caused by bacteria, stress aggravates them. Remember that increase in gastric acid production provided by your friend cortisol? Yep. Not helping. Especially when it's triggered multiple times daily.

These conditions are often self-induced or self-exacerbated. They're created through habitual, negative thought patterns, unreasonable expectations, and unhealthy lifestyle choices.

You may think that tolerating stress is necessary for your survival; it makes you feel needed, important, connected, alive. And if so, you're likely in good shape. In her TED Talk, Kelly McGonigal uses research to explain why perspective on stress matters. People who perceived stress as bad had a higher mortality rate than those who viewed stress as good or helpful.

Threshold

I'm Kelly's type of stress person, the kind who ups my game when I'm under pressure. To me, stress is a straight-shooting friend, "Let's go, Van. Your window of opportunity is closing fast. I'm going to kick your slacker ass this week because I love you, and I know you are a maker of magic!" But every mom has her threshold. Between raising kids and building a business, I've admittedly experienced high levels of cortisol output. It's not hard to recognize when I'm *too* stressed.

The first thing that goes is always my schedule. I forget to pick up kids, I fall asleep at 8pm and then wake up at 4am, I double book commitments… things that, in addition to stressed, make me feel panicked in the moment the offense is realized or committed.

Second stress signal: my body revolts. That pretty middle-aged lady on the book cover? She gets hemorrhoids when she's stressed. *Why, cortisol? Why always my butt?* As if it wasn't enough to get them after birthing my babies, the hemorrhoids have to show up after a long day at the office, too. Awesome.[8] The party doesn't stop at hemorrhoids; stress also makes my heart feel tight, even when I'm sitting down doing nothing.

Instead of surrendering to *OMG, I'm going to die of heart disease,* I roll back my shoulders and take long, deep breaths in through the nose, out through the mouth. While doing this, I close my eyes and visualize white healing light entering my body through the heart space and expanding throughout my heart and chest.

If you are a good visualizer, try employing white light when you're overwhelmed—or even when you feel physically ill. You can add a layer to the practice by imagining your out breath a murky color, releasing energy that doesn't serve you. As it exits your mouth, the white light that surrounds you transmutes it into Love immediately, and you can inhale that next gorgeous white breath.

---

[8]On days when my mindfulness practice forgets to protect my rear end, I usually turn to spiritually based healing. Once, my hemorrhoid and I attended a group sound healing session led by my wildly gifted friend Brian. Halfway through the session, he placed a big Tibetan bowl on my root chakra and made slashing noises with his mouth. As he chanted, I felt that sore break away and move through my left bum cheek, then straight out of my left hip. I ran to the bathroom after the healing, and guess what? It was gone.

I also find it helpful to do a quick body scan the moment you notice the stress or panic and say silently, *Everything works out for me.*

What will happen, if you work with light or breath or body scan consistently, is that instead of getting drowned by cortisol, you'll float on its surface, and then eventually, you'll see that slippery shit when it's rising and yank down the floodgate in time to spare yourself some insanity and even perhaps some hemorrhoids.

And here's more good news. It's not too late to reverse some of the chaos that cortisol production created in your body and mind. Those dead cells in your hippocampus? They'll grow back. Those pimples and cysts? They'll go away. That ulcer? It'll heal. Depression? You can get through it. But not if you keep doing the same habitual baloney you've been doing. To create beneficial change, you need to eliminate the stressful conditions you've created or at least learn how to live above the circumstances you're stuck with.

The Dalai Lama says, "World peace begins with inner peace." He's saying, *Listen, y'all. You just do you. Fix your life. Deal with your drama. Everything else will fall into place around you.* Earth is a stressful place. Threats of terror and destruction pierce daily life. As an individual, you don't have time or resources to fix the trillions of problems created by the human race. **Instead of taking on the burden of healing humanity's collective disaster, you have permission to just work on healing yourself.** Be the drop that inspires the ripple. Be the change you wish to see. Do your inner work so you can deliver your best to others in need in a way that feels healthy and cortisol-appropriate.

It's during intense skirmishes, like the one I had with Xavier, when our kids go freaky-deaky and we are devoid of patience, that we can use the finer points of mindfulness practice and capitalize on

133

the opportunity to make a liberating choice and model composure. We flex the brain muscle and become stronger in the ever-expanding space that exists in one long exhale.

The hope is that eventually the kiddos will follow suit—not right away, but in time. So long as we deliver teachable moments, it will happen. The key is to be consistent, even when consistency is uncomfortable.

Chapter Summary:
May I be protected. May you be protected. May we be protected.

Your mindfulness practice does not protect you from being human, but it does protect your brain from suffering unnecessarily. Chances are there are times when you feel pretty darn stressed out, making it hard to manage time, emotions, and even your physical body.

You have control over more parts of your body than you think, as is proven by research backed by the University of Massachusetts Center for Mindfulness, saying that mindfulness can reduce your active cortisol production by 30%. Let the research fuel your belief in the value of your insight practice, let it help you prioritize a daily commitment to formal meditation. Use triggers in your environment to support your memory.

This does not mean you can't be vehemently, vociferously, violently, verily pissed off or frustrated. But pissed off and frustrated don't help us find solutions. So go ahead and scream. Cry in the shower. Bench-press a hundred pounds. Devour a sleeve of raw cookie dough (mindfully). Feel your pain completely and do whatever it is you do to express yourself. And once you've released the charge, invite breath and awareness. Then listen. Composure will soon come, and it will protect you from unhealthy doses of cortisol.

Journal Prompts:

- How does your body respond to stress? Can you remember a particularly stressful time in your life? Where did it hit you? How did you manage it? What lesson did you take away from it?

- How often do you feel really stressed? Once a day? Once a week? Is it always triggered by the same thing? Is there something you can do that you haven't thought of to completely remove yourself from that stress? What is required, besides courage, to make changes that would protect your body from stress?

- Remember a time when stress helped you motivate. What was that like?

16

May I be present. May you be present. May we be present.

Here

This whole "first me" idea implies that there is an orderly process to mood and brood management that we parents can follow linearly. As if *this* happens *then that* happens *then* we are happy. As if we figure out all of our bullshit in a way we can actually understand and even measure… and *then* we pivot toward our children, full of wisdom and confidence, dropping enlightenment bombs with each loving interaction. *As if.*

The truth of mindful parenting isn't a chronological one, nor is it something we can necessarily quantify. It's more nonlinear and mysterious.

Present moment surrender heightens awareness, supporting our ability to be more discerning in our behavior. Our healthy present moment choices put us on a happier timeline. Through this, we release future yuck and past yuck, and our babies benefit immediately, shifting in real time to a higher version of themselves as they experience more peaceful moments with us. We see evidence of mutual evolution, ascending with and through each other. There's an exchange happening between parent and child that feels juicy and loving, even enlightening.

Gary Zukav writes in his book, *The Seat of the Soul*, "…if our actions create harmony and empowerment in another, we also will come to feel that harmony and empowerment." When we engage mindfulness, a lovely shift in our state of consciousness can occur—a wholeness, or perhaps a wholesomeness, a kindness to ourselves and others.

As parents, we have countless opportunities to exercise mutual enlightenment. Conscious parenting expert Shefali Tsabary poetically calls these opportunities "a meeting of souls." Without saying a word, our presence of being tells our babies that we are here for them and that they are loved. The healing manifests in a little ball of Metta that bounces back and forth between us.

Presence sounds like such a simple act, but so often we find ourselves mentally checked out. We sit in a meeting at work and our mind wanders to weekend plans. Our son recounts his soccer match and we're wondering how long this play-by-play will go on because we've got carrots to peel. We anticipate the next beginning, only to get there and start waiting for the end.

We're here but we're not totally *here*.

Presence provides us with greater capacity to process stimuli. When we engage our five senses in the present, we notice more. If our mind is focused on the immediate surroundings, chances are there's less mental clutter to clog up our reception. A fully present listener can better process sound, inflection, emotions, and nonverbal cues, and our counterparts feel genuinely heard.

In full-presence mode, we may feel more grateful, more joyful, more receptive, more compassionate. We may also feel relieved. *You mean I don't have to multitask? It's alright for me to do just this one thing, and doing just this one thing is a perfectly good reason not to engage in all those other things at the same time? Sign me up!*

Okay, more reality checking. Doing just one thing is nearly impossible. This is especially true for parents. Most of us are straddling two worlds: the one that revolves around family, and the one that revolves around work. For some moms, those two worlds nestle cozily together; being a full-time mom *is* our work and calling. Some are born to flourish in motherly love, packing healthy lunch boxes with passion, organizing closets with efficiency and pleasure, burping babies with absolute presence of being. Work and family are tucked neatly in one basket. As someone who was a stay-at-home mom for my first 10 years of motherhood, I can attest it wasn't easy, but it was a more focused, streamlined existence.

For other moms, though, the roads of work and family intersect very little, or not at all. There's an unspoken struggle, a ubiquitous guilt, a ceaseless pressure, making us feel like we can't give ourselves over completely to anything. We deliver our best knowing it's not *really* our best, but the best version of ourselves available given our situation.

100%

My own affliction with half-assed motherhood peaked in the summer of 2012. When I placed a sleeve of Saltines on the counter next to a jar of soy butter at dinnertime, I knew it was time for me to re-examine my workload and my priorities. In response, I decided that for one entire summer, I'd *just* be a mom. I started by vanquishing a fully present parent's ultimate nemeses: social media. I turned off my YouTube account and logged off Twitter, ignored my Gmail inbox and steered clear of Facebook. I also put my writing and teaching and energy-workshop-taking on hold. Instead, I cleaned the house and folded laundry, planted gardens, and provided three square meals a day. I broke up fights and yelled at kids, demanded submission and rewarded compliance. I packed sandy beach bodies into my trusty Ford and played Ghost in the Graveyard after dusk.

I was 100% mommy.

Some good, some mediocre, but 100% nonetheless.

While I admittedly went a little crazy in the land of board games, Top 40 radio, and double scoops of peppermint ice cream, being a completely tuned-in, uninterruptable parent allowed me to release that chronic feeling of incompletion and guilt. *Aaahhhhhh!*

Not everyone can easily take the summer off, but our babies can still feel well attended and well loved, knowing that when we're in the room with them physically, we're also in the room with them mentally and emotionally. The time given by a parent working outside the home can be equal in quality to time invested by those working inside the home if we parent with full presence.

To do that, it's important that you spend a few quiet minutes getting centered in the space between your two worlds. Even five minutes of self-care can help you release the passionate-person-with-dreams-and-to-do-lists and welcome in the wholly-present-parent-with-gobs-of-love-and-patience you know you can be.

A meditational transition can help you shift gears from then to now, logging out of the virtual world, reprioritizing the rat race, clearing space for your family and their need for your focused attention.

So, each day as you return home from work, hide out for a few minutes and meditate. Arriving into the moment may take effort. There are a few different tricks that can help you get there. Combine them or pick one favorite. Any effort will do.

Come to your senses. Help establish yourself in the present moment by tuning into your senses, one at a time. Start with your sense of sight. Look around your space. Don't judge, just see what's there for you. When you feel safe and comfortable with your surroundings, close your eyes and tune into your sense of sound. Recognize sounds that pop up without searching for them. Just let them arrive and pass. Next, shift focus to your sense of smell. Is it pleasant? Unpleasant? Somewhere in between? Become aware of your sense of taste, taking note of flavor in your mouth, noticing any judgment or maybe a craving. Finally settle into your sense of touch. Your hands are a great point of entry. Sense their position, temperature, connection to each other or even buzzing sensation. Sit quietly in your *now* energy.

Drop your breath. Use intention to shift your breath from your chest to your belly. Notice the process you experience in making that shift; perhaps your breath stalls out around the diaphragm. Maybe you notice that your waist and back expand and contract with your breath. Slowly make your breath deeper. Breathing in, the belly rises, breathing out, the belly falls.

Take five breaths. Take five deep breaths, in through the nose so that your lungs feel completely satisfied, and out through the mouth, long and relaxed. Once you get to five, welcome normal breathing, in and out through the nose, and take another five. And another. Keep counting your breaths.

Welcome white light. Close your eyes and imagine a white orb hovering above your head. Fill it with the intention of healing and love. Invite it to drop in through your crown and imagine it lighting up each part of your body as it slowly makes its way to your toes.

Zip up your spine. Plant your rear end into a chair. Imagine a golden zipper at your tailbone and zip up your spine from root to crown. As the zipper rises, illuminate your spine in gold, gently squeezing your shoulder blades together, rolling your shoulders back and down so that you create lots of space between your shoulders and your ears. With a strong back and open heart, extend the crown of your head toward the sky and tuck your chin slightly. Relax your arms, letting them drape down the sides of your body, then open your hands and place them palms up on your lap. Maintaining posture, rock side to side and back to front a few times to find your center. If you'd like to take this meditation a step further, imagine that your golden spine is a diffuser and send a golden healing mist throughout your body.

If your technique is not inviting, you'll never do it, so pick something that feels good and is easy. Your transitional meditation can take place in your parked car, in a nearby green space, by the water, on a sidewalk bench, on your front stoop, or in the lobby of your building. Just be sure to meditate *before* you greet your kids, so the second they lay eyes on you, you are all theirs. When children feel this kind of assurance, even if you only see them for 20 minutes before bedtime, there is nothing to feel guilty about.

I'll be the first to admit, there are days I don't make that transition. Here's where mindfulness plays in: I *know* I'm not making a transition from entrepreneur to mommy and I offer myself a little Metta forgiveness for the lapse in presence. I also cop to my shortcomings, "Kids, I'm floundering right now. I'm not in my right head. Can you please give me a parenting pass today?"

Like I said, I *work toward* fully present parenting in my home. There are plenty of times when I can't pull myself together, days when the kids are hammering me with repetitive questions, moments I feel a sudden urge to smash my head into a wall. I have to notice when I become unconscious zombie-mom and drag myself back to presence. No one said this would be easy. Presence takes effort, vigilance. I have to fight my reactive desire to tune out, to scream, to swat, to hide, to demand, to blame, to avoid, to give them a screen— all of the unconscious behaviors that reflect old habits.

Mindfulness doesn't erase those habits; it just allows us to remember that those urges aren't who we are and helps us recognize the potentially complicated consequences of those urges.

It seems so basic, doesn't it? To be present? To be aware? To be here now? Sometimes I cannot believe how many books I've read on mindfulness or the hundreds of hours I've spent learning or teaching about this practice, or how hard I have had to work to undo what I've done. The volume and intensity of all this effort motivates me to make healthy decisions every present-moment chance I get, because this practice is anything but basic.

Chapter Summary:
May I be present. May you be present. May we be present.

A few years back, my sister-in-law Annie and I sat with Thich Nhat Hanh, who was doing a dharma talk at Boston's famous Trinity Church in Back Bay. Annie and I both loved him and were regular pebble meditation practitioners. We had front row seats. It was really special. At the end of the talk, we shopped the bookstore and found a treasure trove of handwritten calligraphies penned by Thay himself. We carefully considered which to bring home. She went with "mountain solid," complete with his signature circle around the two words. I really wanted one with that circle, too, but when I flipped to the words "I know you are there and I am happy," my eyes stung with tears. I bought it, framed it, and hung the calligraphy where everyone could see it and be reminded that I was there for them. I desperately wanted to feel that someone was there for me, too. We all want to be loved, validated, seen, understood. This is what full presence can provide for someone without having to say a word.

Journal Prompts:
- You have dozens of tools in your mental health toolbox now. Some are conceptual, some are lifestyle changes you can make, and some are just tiny shifts in perception. In your journal, make three columns with the headings "Concept,"

"Lifestyle," and "Perception" and categorize some of your tools. As your practice develops, be sure to be pulling from each column. This provides a multi-layered experience of mindfulness practice and helps to bring a little bit more understanding to that which sometimes seems random and chaotic.

- What do you currently do to transition at the end of your day? Is there anything you dread as you approach home after a long day of work? If you are a stay-at-home mom, is there anything that sucks you out of the present moment? Are there any tools you can use to help you stay grounded?

17

May I speak. May you speak. May we speak.

Squabbling

Several winters ago, a perfectly uncomfortable parenting moment unfolded before my eyes. The kids and I suited up for a gorgeous powder ski day. We have a home near Mount Sunapee in New Hampshire and the kids have skied there almost every winter weekend since they could walk. The mountain feels like our backyard. On this day in particular, they behaved like it actually was our backyard.

While waiting in the thickest bit of the Sunapee Express lift line, Xavier stabbed at Scarlett with his ski pole. My superfast mommy reflexes seized the weapon just before impalement. While I congratulated myself on avoiding a trip to the infirmary, Xavier thrashed and sobbed and begged for his poles back. He immediately melted into a miserable puddle of expensive leisure equipment and brightly colored technical fabric.

While I was distracted by Xavi's fit, Penelope and Scarlett started to argue. It was a heated she said/she said about *wah-wah-wah*, made more intense by the volume required for them to hear each other through thickly padded POC helmets and their brother's wails. Before I knew it, the debate escalated to a brawl and Scarlett threw down her signature fighting tactic: the dreaded *shrieking eel cry*. (If you've ever seen *Princess Bride*, you know the sound.)

The whole world stopped.

Eighty pairs of close-range eyes shot toward my blaring, neon family.

After a fight-flight-freeze moment (cue amygdala), I remembered my mindfulness practice (fire up hippocampus) and decided to be my authentic self without apology (hello prefrontal cortex), which meant taking a deep breath and mindfully disciplining them in that densely packed crowd exactly the same way I would at home (goodbye cortisol). While Xavi moaned and clung to my shins, I popped out of my skis and squatted down between the girls.

"Hug it out, women," I said in my best loving-mommy-meets-no-nonsense-army-guy voice. "Two minutes. Now. Go."

"Mommy, we're in the ski line."

"Mom, I am not doing that here."

"You're bringing all of your yuck into these people's lives and it's not okay. Especially on a powder day." I pulled my gloves off with my teeth, fished an iPhone from my pocket, and let my chilled index finger hover over the stopwatch on the screen, while the girls begrudgingly pivoted their ski tips toward each other inch by awkward inch. Xavier rolled off my ski boot to make room for them, his anger and uncooperativeness suddenly replaced by amusement and compliance. The sisters shuffled close, skis alternating, boots and helmets crunching, mittened hands searching to connect around each other's backs.

My finger tapped "start" and they hugged.

And they hugged.

And they rolled their eyes behind their goggles.

And they looked weird.

And they hugged some more.

Ahead of us, the line scooched forward while P and S stood

locked together stiffly in place, like oversized action figures. The folks behind us would just have to wait.

As the Love silently healed my girls' anger, their little bodies relaxed into something that looked almost comfortable. The energy in the space surrounding my family shifted. Instead of scowling, onlookers began to smile. (This is the brain's mirror neurons hard at work here, adopting my girls' softening emotions just by bearing witness to them.) When the clock timed out, the sisters untangled from each other's arms, laughing, relaxed, and renewed.

Mindfulness-induced miracle achieved.

As we shuffled toward the lift, a young woman tapped my shoulder and said, "I'm totally going to remember that for when I'm a mom. I've never seen anything like it before. I can't believe that worked. I love it!" I laughed and thanked her for the best compliment I'd gotten all year. I told her it worked because hugging triggers a physiological change in the body, but it takes 90 seconds to happen. I make my kids hug for two minutes because I'm a strict disciplinarian.

Of course, we don't always end up on a peaceful chairlift ride to the mountaintop. There are times when we are trapped so deep in a blizzard of misbehavior that the summit might as well be the moon, times when we leave the mountain altogether and drag ourselves home in defeat, times when we say and do things we regret—things that are hurtful, things we judge and are judged harshly for. But when we reflect on our ugliest interactions mindfully, with forgiveness, openness, and trust, we upgrade mistakes to lessons. **These experiences are not here to break us, they're here to inform our next choices.**

We invite mindfulness the instant we realize we're lost; it's here that we avoid the rocky, rutted neural pathway between our amygdala and our prefrontal cortex and create fresh tracks, tips pointed in the direction of the peaceful valley below.

Oversharing

Generally speaking, my kids are selfish communicators. They demand my attention whether I'm ready to give it or not. They then jabber for 15 minutes without taking a breath. "Can I say something?" is the most commonly spoken question in my home.

At age 27, Chelsea has graduated from holding our ears hostage, but my younger set is in the thick of it. Penelope over-talks her siblings, Scarlett speaks in feelings rather than truths, and Xavi explains every video game he plays and every book he reads with such grueling specificity our eyes roll back in our heads and we foam at the mouth, and then when one of us thinks he's done and tries to chime in he barks, "Wait! I'm not finished yet!"

One day, my mother-in-law, Landy, and I were sitting together in the kitchen having brunch when Scarlett came over to tell us about a book she was reading. Full plot. Lots of twists. Hard to follow. Honestly, I was not interested in hearing about this book. But with my mother-in-law watching, I was on my best behavior. I put my fork down, gave her my full attention, and held eye contact until the story was over.

Landy is a brilliant and respected psychotherapist. She lectured worldwide on a healing technique called Transactional Analysis for many years before she retired at age 82. She is incredibly observant and often shares her thoughts, praiseful or meh, on my parenting practices. In true therapist fashion, she folded her hands on her lap, set her jaw, and patiently observed us.

After Scarlett left the room, Landy congratulated me on my parenting then said she remembered a day, a lifetime ago, when young Michael was pestering her, eager to recount a *Gilligan's Island* episode in great detail. At the time, Landy had been chatting with a friend and dismissed her son. Her friend stopped the conversation and said, "Landy, if you don't listen when he talks about the little things, he won't talk to you about the big things." It was a profound lesson in compassionate listening for Landy, and it has become one for me as well.

I know that listening patiently is the right thing to do, but that doesn't mean it's easy to do it. Fortunately, many years ago I was introduced to mindful communication practice through a curriculum called *Mindfulness-Based Stress Reduction* (MBSR). MBSR is a course offered through the Center for Mindfulness at UMass Amherst Medical School. Teachers devote a good portion of the course syllabus to mindful communication, during which students sit in dyads and learn how to listen and respond to each other with compassion. This is an effective technique to implement when kids are fighting (more on that later), but it's also a good way to stop the story locomotive and teach kids how to take turns in a healthy conversation. Here is my mommy adaptation of some skills I picked up through the MBSR program:

1. Look into your child's eyes.
2. Set an internal timer for two minutes and invite him to tell his story without interrupting, checking your phone, or looking away.
3. When your mommy clock goes off, gently interrupt, and tell him two or three things about his story you found interesting.
4. Ask him if there's anything he wants to add.
5. Listen patiently while he responds for another minute or so.
6. Repeat back one thing you thought was really cool.
7. Ask if he'd like to hear your perspective.
8. Pause, then share. Limit your story to two minutes.
9. Pause and wait.

10. Ask your child if he thinks anything you said sounded interesting then invite him to follow steps four through six.

Fighting

Using mindful communication while storytelling is a fab warm-up act for using it during verbal skirmishes. It took me a long time to figure how to fight fair. It's not something my sisters and I learned as kids. We battled daily, but the only thing our parents ever told us to do was STOOOPPPPP FIIIIGHTIIIINNNNNNNGGGG!!!! My parents were married for 19 years and *never* fought in front of us kids. Needless to say, their divorce came as huge shock to me; but moreover, I didn't know adults actually fought. I thought screaming matches were a kid thing that we'd eventually grow out of. How wrong I was.

One afternoon, years ago, Michael and I got into a heated argument in front of the kids. It started spontaneously with a little snippiness over a pair of smelly sneakers then quickly escalated into something more complicated. We sat down and hashed it out relatively mindfully while the kids circled silently and watched. After five minutes or so of debate, we apologized to each other for getting hot over something so silly and moved on with our day.

People fight. That's life. A family brawl is a great opportunity to model mindful communication and teach by example. Our young audience reminds us to keep it clean—take turns listening to each other, acknowledge our partner's frustration, express compassion for our partner's pain. This is healthy!

It's okay to fight in front of kids, so long as we make up in front of them. When our kids see us argue mindfully, they learn how to argue mindfully. And when they see us apologize and forgive, they learn how to apologize and forgive. It's okay to be mad, it's okay to argue, it's okay to be wrong, it's okay to forgive, and it's okay to move on.

When I lead youth workshops, "fighting fair" is one of my favorite exercises; and it is well received by students. The exercise translates easily into home life. There is so much violence and suffering happening around the world, over which we have zero control; but here in our homes, we do have control. When we realize this, we can work toward establishing peace where it counts the most.

When I coach my own children through fighting fair, arguments diffuse quickly. Not sometimes—always. One night at home, my girls were arguing over screen time. They were sharing an iPad, making music videos upstairs while I was downstairs watching a documentary on the Holocaust—not in the mood to be disrupted by battling children. One would stomp downstairs and complain, then stomp back up. Then the other would stomp downstairs and do the same. When they both appeared together, I paused my documentary and turned on Metta Mom. With minimal effort, the girls stopped fighting in under five minutes. This is how we did it:

Penelope was a little less emotional, so I had her be the listener first. Scarlett expressed her side of the story in full color while Penelope held her eye contact. Scarlett spoke only to Penelope, not to me. Any time she turned to me for approval or support, I'd direct her back to Penelope, keeping the focus just between them. She knew she had time to fully express, without being cut off or discounted. No rush. She only took a minute or two to get through her story, and then I asked Penelope to repeat back exactly what Scarlett had said. She did.

"Scarlett, did Penelope miss anything? Is there anything you want to add?" She shook her head.

"Okay, now it's Penelope's turn."

She spoke while Scarlett listened and looked. Then Scarlett

repeated exactly what Penelope had said. Penelope felt heard and understood and did not need to add anything else.

We decided that the girls simply had two different perspectives, neither bad nor wrong, and they still wanted to create something special together. That was it. I pressed play and returned to my documentary while the girls made videos. Peacefully.

I know it's not always this simple. Sometimes this process might take several rounds before reaching a truce. Also, your kids might be physical fighters, which would require some creative logistics. If your kids tend to get in each other's faces, hit, scratch, pinch, punch, or pull hair, establish boundaries and appropriate distance with a yoga mat. Have one child sit at each end of the mat, facing each other. They are close enough that they have to share space, but far enough apart that they aren't in pummeling proximity.

Cursing

Sometimes I holler mindfully. That's right: holler mindfully. For dramatic impact. I use my volume as a tool of consciousness. Sometimes I even swear mindfully. Mark Twain had my back on this one when he wrote, "Under certain circumstances, profanity provides a relief denied even to prayer." It sounds perverse, but I've got to say, a rare, well-timed, passionately delivered curse word is shockingly effective in getting kids to clam up and listen. They're like, *Wow, Mommy swore. This is wild. Let's be quiet and listen. Maybe she'll do it again.*

Mindful swearing is like eating a Boston Cream doughnut. One every six months or so is a surprising break from the norm, but weekly, or worse, daily and ingestion diminishes its magical powers and makes you feel gross. Trust me, I know from experience. The first time I broke the profanity seal with my kids was highly effective. I actually hid a smile and mini-fist-pumped as I walked away from their silent, stunned faces. About a year later, I tried it again, and again found great success. I ran into trouble soon after, though, because four-letter words frequent my daily adult dialogue. It became very hard to control my usage, and I started dropping at least one *shit* or *fuck* every month. I crossed the line and it started making my kids feel insecure. So I don't swear intentionally anymore, just by accident. If you have more self-control than I do, I say go for it.

Not my finest parenting tip, but I'm not a doctor and this book is about reality, not rhetoric. When I've got multiple children melting down, the F-bomb, used sparingly, is a terrific tradeoff for a dead silent room. The point is, I'm engaging in shocking behavior, and I know it. I'm aware that I am teaching my children naughty language. I'm aware I'm making them uncomfortable. But I'm not judging myself for it. I'm using the emotional heat available to me in the moment to cool my brood.

Now that the kids are older, the cursing has lost some of its power. They've heard it all at this point so now my potty mouth serves as an invitation for them to cuss back, which makes my skin crawl.

My girls are as tall as I am, and Xavier is not far behind. Carrying them to time out and physically peeling them apart during wrestling matches are no longer options. This is why it's important to teach them how to fight while they're young. It will not only spare you years of frustration, it will further establish your home as sacred space where people feel honored, heard, and happy. As your children grow, this communication skill grows with them. They can use it with siblings, friends, and eventually co-workers and partners. Practicing mindful communication is like putting out little fires everywhere they go. When the world is burning up, like ours is now, every little bit helps.

As curious students of our own inner wisdom, as vigilant practitioners, as receptive listeners, we can approach the world with mental health, genuine kindness, deep compassion, and loving intention. Even when our carefully framed images of perfection are smashed to bits on the stairs, even when everyone in the lift line looks at us like we've lost our minds, we can press on knowing that our *radical acts of sanity*[9] are spinning us face to face with love, inch by awkward inch.

Each one of us contributes to the sanity of the world. Each one of us is naturally empowered to heal our mind and inspire healing in those around us. Don't believe otherwise. Depression, anger, perfectionism, judgment, obsession, worry, confusion, competition, stress, despair... these are sufferings we accumulate from birth and shoulder through life, all miscreated out of fear.

Chapter Summary:
> *May I speak. May you speak. May we speak.*

Mindful communication is rooted in your ability to protect yourself from panic, to stay grounded in the present moment, and to stay fiercely peaceful in your mind and body. See how the chapters are building in this section? One exercise informs the next. When you fuse these practices together, you earn superhero status and can rule the world (inside your house).

Any superhero will attest that being peaceful is not synonymous with being a pushover. Sometimes the best thing you can do to maintain peace is to get fierce.

There isn't a mother alive who hasn't experienced her own wit's end. When you feel yours approaching, feel it all the way and

---

[9]This is John Kabat-Zinn's famous phrase from the intro of his book *Full Catastrophe Living.*

use that fire to ignite your disciplinary power or your listening power or your quiet power. Be creative. Be real. Be the high-vibing badass you know you are.

Do what works, even if it's weird.

Journal Prompts:

- Search your mind for a time that you disciplined your children with such skill you sat back after and smiled. What made that experience so effective? How long did it take? Was it hard for you? Was there part of the experience that made you uncomfortable? What was required of your mental state to engage this kind of super-powered parenting?
- Now search your mind for a time that you lost your temper, struck your child, screamed and swore, or engaged in disciplinary action fueled by rage. Did the tactic work? What can you say about the amount of physical and emotional energy it took to engage this technique? Did it take more time or less time than the super-powered way? How did you recover and how did that process feel?
- Do you discipline with words or with action? Are different approaches necessary for different children?
- How do you deal with discipline when you're in public? When friends are over? When you're with extended family? Do you up your game or let things slide? Why or why not?
- When you fight with your spouse do you hide? How do you handle fights between your kids? Do you fight with your kids? Why?
- Exploring movies and books with your kids establishes common ground, which is a great way to engage fun conversation where everyone has equal footing and valid

opinions. Try watching a series like *The Avengers* with the kids and spark some healthy banter. Give lots of space for kids to disagree with you and still feel empowered. Also write down what you learn from your kids.

18

May I be juicy. May you be juicy. May we be juicy.

Peaches

"The privilege of a lifetime is to become who you really are," Carl Jung said. Close your eyes and take it in for a minute. You are designed to walk a Path, and you are responsible for stepping into your fullest experience of authentic self without apology. **Who are you to deny the world of your God-given gifts?**

Your personal awakening may cause discomfort for people who are not living authentically themselves, be they your children, your parents, or your next-door neighbors. Another person's discomfort with your intentional, love-based decisions cannot be the filter for your decisions and desires.

A modern burlesque dancer named Dita Von Teese said, "You can be the ripest, juiciest peach in the world. And there's still going to be somebody who hates peaches." First of all, not everyone is going to be your superfan. Even if you are the kindest person in the world, you're still going to have haters, just because you are you. And second, a peach can only be a peach. It doesn't ask permission to be a peach. It doesn't wish it were a banana or a kiwi. It accepts that it's a peach and it does its best to grow big and ripe. People are just the same. Your job is to be the very best possible version of yourself, without apology and without asking permission, and know that your talents and strengths are valuable, meaningful, and impactful.

Our children assume authenticity on day one. By day two, the world is already trying to convince them that they are not okay the way they are. We parents must take care to treasure, nurture, and preserve their divine uniqueness, reminding them that it is *only* okay to be the way they are. We must allow them space and permission to comfortably grow into their fullest, juiciest potential. With a little less judging, a little less directing, and a lot more observing, we parents can tap into this extraordinary source of authenticity and be inspired. Next time you see your child playing uninhibitedly, creating intently, laughing unselfconsciously, or dancing wildly, stop and bear witness to a ripe, juicy peach dangling from your very own tree.

This is not to say we should let them run wild; but using mindful observation—observation *without judgment*—and detaching from our personal hang-ups and expectations allows our kiddos ample space to explore safely. A great example most parents can relate to is the way children express themselves while getting dressed each day.

Dressed

Style is the way we present to the world. It's the ultimate first impression. Clothing, accessories, hair, and physique tell family, friends, peers, and strangers, *This is how I roll. This is what I want you to know about me right off the bat.*

When Chelsea was little, her clothing choices inspired hot debate. From early on, she expressed herself unapologetically through high heels, short skirts, and purple lipstick. When she was about nine, Michael and I took her to a Britney Spears concert at the Boston Garden (or whatever it was called that year). On that blustery January evening in New England, Chels bounded downstairs wearing a sleeveless belly shirt and Daisy Dukes. Her long hair was crimped and explosive; her face glowed with violet glitter.

As stepmom, I clamped my mouth shut, but Michael directed her back up to her room "You're not wearing that. Go upstairs and change." You can imagine the conversation that followed. We've all been there, be it with our four-year-old who wants to wear a Batman costume to church or our 16-year-old trying to sneak out for a date in our Louboutins. (Okay, so I don't own Louboutins, but if I did, my kids would totally want to snatch them.) If memory serves, the pre-concert compromise with Chelsea was a pair of ripped jeans and a warm coat over all that exposed skin.

Setting limits is important. Kids need them. We just don't want to squash their self-expression by way of subjective censoring. Michael and Nancy were always great about this with Chelsea. She had lots of freedom to decide how she'd present to the world, and she grew into an amazing, expressive, confident, mature, authentic adult.

I, however, learned this parenting lesson the hard way.

When Penelope first started going to school, I would dress her up in the most adorable outfits. She was my little doll. Sometimes she would stand in her closet with me as I considered this sweater or that headband, and she'd dare to make suggestions. "Oh no, honey," I'd say, "You just wore that yesterday." Or, "Penelope, it's February. Too cold for a sundress." Or even worse, "No, Sweetpea, that doesn't match."

I'd become The Style Nazi. *No style for you!*

I'd soon learn that playing fashion police results in a sad, sad fate. By first grade, Penelope became a little monster in the morning. She was unable to pick out her own clothes, but also rejected everything I suggested. Literally, I would lay five looks on her bed and she'd hate them all. She would cry and scream, I would cry and scream… over clothes. Just clothes.

Ugh.

Her tantrums (and mine) were totally my fault. I never allowed her to express herself through fashion (which is so *not just clothes*!) and she didn't know who she was stylistically. Lesson learned. Now at age 14, Miss Penelope has grown out of her wardrobe resistance. Like many children, she cycles through fashion phases: the slouchy hat phase, the all-black phase, the hipster phase, the athleisure phase… and now I know my job is to zip my lip and applaud her through it all.

As the family grew, my desire to play dress-up dwindled. There was just no time to fuss over clothes. The kids were lucky if they had clean socks. On our most pathetic wardrobe days, my crew would go to school wearing the putty-colored hospital-issued scrunch socks I wore home after giving birth.

For those reasons, in stark contrast to her tortured sister, Scarlett was always allowed to dress as she pleased. *Express away, dear Scarlett!* When she was little, I'd await her descent each morning, eager to see how she'd wow the world. She would sashay into the kitchen dressed like Punky Brewster one day and the late Marilyn Reisman the next (Google her). Unflappably proud of the way she looked, this child was not one bit worried if I, or others, loved it or hated it.

In elementary school, Scarlett's every ensemble was a toe to tip masterpiece. My all-time favorite: silver sparkly sneakers, jaguar print tights, green and orange sequin camouflage skirt, lacy pink striped blouse, furry fuchsia vest, all topped with a silver beret. As my friend Doreen, a talented fashion consultant, once said, "Scarlett's got all the makings of a fashionista. Color, texture, and shine!"

As an adolescent, my bold middle child wears thick black eyeliner and grunge concert t-shirts. She's expressive and brave. She's not worried about people judging her. Scarlett's wardrobe choices bring me great joy in the morning. Authenticity without apology. Pure *flow*. She Is who she Is. And who am I to judge anyway?

Three kids down and one to go. Xavier may be a boy, but he cares about personal expression through clothes, too. Well, at least he used to. If it were up to him, he would have gone to every day of second grade in a two-sizes-too-small black sweat suit screen printed with skeleton bones. Seriously, he loved that get-up. Unfairly, tiny skeleton pants were not okay with me.

Even though I was much looser with stylistic choices by this point in my motherhood, I did and do believe there was real value in dressing respectfully for school. For his first couple years of elementary school, he was allowed to wear (non-skeleton) sweatpants only if he paired them with a button-down collar shirt. He was obsessed with animals, so we compromised with animal graphic t-shirts over the button-downs. Once a week, I'd let him wear whatever he wanted, no rules.

The animal shirts were awesome because he was a bit of a nature savant. By age seven, he had a stack of animal encyclopedias memorized and was known to monitor birds and bugs in the yard for hours on end, opting for *Nat Geo* documentaries and *Wild Kratts* episodes over superheroes or sports. He could not get enough of critters. His animal shirts were and sometimes still are conversation starters for him, ways to share his authenticity with others. As a little guy, he'd point at the iguana on his chest and rattle off a dozen facts about tropical habitats, mating rituals, biological defenses, and eating preferences.

At age 10, Xavi still loves sweatpants that are several sizes too small. He wears the same clothes to school and to bed three days in a row and refuses to brush his hair.

Rarely do I appreciate it.

Sometimes it makes me cringe.

Frequently I bite my tongue as he leaves the house in the morning.

I find peace knowing I did my best to guide him when he was impressionable, and now he's his own boss. I'm assuming his choices will change when he notices girls.

Fashion may be a superficial example of a child's authentic expression, but it's also universal, and that's why I chose these stories to share. Our kids express themselves in countless ways, whether it's through the way they dress, the passions they pursue, or the lifestyle choices they make. We parents are privileged to bear witness to the first sparks of their unique potential, even though at times it surely looks crude and weird to us.

We may look at our kids as if they are aliens, wondering, *Where did this obsession with mustaches come from? Is it necessary that every shade of pink is represented in your hair color? What the hell is so funny about Charlie the Unicorn?* But it's important that we keep our opinions to ourselves so that they can explore their authenticity freely and grow into the ripest, juiciest peaches they can possibly be.

We all know the Golden Rule: *Do unto others as you would have them do unto you.* If we wish to be observed without judgment of our body, speech, and mind, then it only makes sense to observe our children's body, speech, and mind without judgment as well. By committing to the Golden Rule, we can feel as comfortable with their authenticity as we feel with our own. We can accept them as they are.

Chapter Summary:

May I be juicy. May you be juicy. May we be juicy.

Every human learns through trial and error; your little darlings included. They can wait until they're 23 and living on their own to take risks and do ridiculous things, or you can give them lots of space to take risks and do ridiculous things while they're safe and protected under your care. That may mean that your child is labeled as weird. That may mean your child is not popular. That may mean that your child screws up big time. That may mean that your child does not think or act the same way you do. That may also mean that your child grows up juicy and badass, knowing who they are, living their Truth without apology and without asking permission.

Journal Prompts:

- We're still building a strong mindful parenting foundation. As we inch from judgment to juice, we bring another wisp of order to this nonlinear glob of spiritual enlightenment. How's this process going for you? Do you feel it? Are there any steps missing for you? What are they? Write them down. Is there anything that's difficult for you? Write that down, too.

- Were you overprotected or conditioned by your parents? Was it helpful? Do you ever feel penned in by expectations? If so, are you repeating this pattern with your own children? Or perhaps do you take it to the opposite extreme? Is there a happy balance where you give your kids freedom and limits? Have you ever written your parameters out? Try it now.

- What techniques, traditions, or habits have you picked up from your own parents that you've passed down to your kids? Are they activities and values that make you happy? Why have you decided continued implementing these behaviors? What's *your* reason?

19

May I practice non-judgment. May you practice non-judgment. May we practice non-judgment.

Sucking

Have you ever experienced a moment in your motherhood when you were like, *Wow, I may have just earned Mother of the Year for (insert caretaking feat here).*

I have. Most of my friends have, too.

As moms, when we stick the landing, we know it and we celebrate it. The jubilee is always cut short, though, because our kids quickly shift into a new phase of life and the parenting skills that we worked so hard to perfect become obsolete.

With age, my children have become more sophisticated, manipulative, and uncompliant. They are able express themselves so colorfully and with such self-awareness, one may believe that these teenagers are also logical and rational. But they aren't always. Their brains aren't developed enough to be. And to top it off, their hormones make them wildly unreasonable. This is the cruel reality of motherhood: just when you think you're doing a bang-up job, your kids remind you that you actually totally suck.

Them: *Mom is totally clueless. She doesn't get it. I'm going to do whatever I want to do because I am the center of the Universe and I know everything.*

Me: *Argh.*

This shift in my daughters' attitudes felt like an ambush. My parenting skill set was still in Cute Little Kid Problem Mode, but my pubescent girls had upgraded to Raging Hormone Problem Mode. While they exploded into young adulthood, I built a mental-emotional dam that blocked my kneejerk reactions to their challenges. I confronted them with silence and projected my best unruffled Buddha face, stifling my natural inclination to toss my own hormones into the mix.

Oh, I was feeling it all on the inside, for sure. My heart and head would pound and squeeze, but my eyes would remain calm and neutral. After a skirmish, I'd retreat to my bedroom and sob into a pillow or bitch about the drama with a friend. This method of parenting was not only ineffective for my maturing gang, but it was also unsustainable for me.

For a good while, my children were fighting daily. DAILY. Twenty minutes of arguing (hollering) would go by and then at minute 21, the dam would burst violently and everything I'd held together would come rushing forth with raging power. I'd go way over the top—yelling, crying, grabbing, and punishing.

We needed help.

Activate

The Universe delivered me Carmen, a brilliant family therapist who taught me that I was waiting too long to engage my superpowers. This clueless mom is a Scorpio, a water sign. My astrological natal chart teems with water: four planets in Scorpio and two in Cancer, which is also a water sign. All this liquid makes me just as you'd imagine a watery person would be: emotional, active, flowing.

"Water needs to flow," Carmen coached me. "Don't wait until the dam breaks to come to life. At the very first sign of misbehavior, you need to pair the force of the dam break with the control of your mindfulness practice to direct your energy and shut down the chaos and assure your kids that regardless of their logic, the behavior is not acceptable."

She nailed it.

I'd been behaving like the Wonder Twin who shape shifts into water and gets carried around in a bucket by his animagus sister. Trapped in the bucket, I was useless, ineffective. It was time to tip the bucket and flood my household with loving action.

Loving action began with envisioning the ideal conditions we wanted to create in the home. The kids and I made a family communication covenant. First, we had to decide which of our current communication habits made us feel good and which habits made us feel bad. The kids chose to start with bad: *mimicking, whining, screaming, tone, negativity, lying, stealing, name-calling, interrupting, badgering, instigating, saying "Shut up."* Long list, right? Clearly, we were in a slump.

Our good list was not as long, more evidence of our need for a new contract: *"Own your beef," be nice, make eye contact, be on time, offer solutions, take turns, include people.* These desirable behaviors became part of our family covenant.

The kids came up with punishments for violating our contract, including getting docked one hour of screen time per transgression.[10] Penelope suggested that I practice delayed discipline. In other words, typically she would mutter icky things about me while retreating to her room post-brawl, and I'd call down the stairs, "That's another hour without your phone. And that's another hour. And that's another hour." Instead, she asked that I allow her space to mutter those things, write her punishment silently on a sticky note,

---

[10]Screen time has been hugely contentious in our house. They think it's a divine right. I think it's a privilege. The ongoing score in Kids v. Mom: 0-0.

and post it on the fridge.

She reasoned, "When I mutter and you keep taking things away from me, it just makes me want to come back and fight with you. And then I get in more trouble. So, if you can let me go, I'll understand the outcome because I'm aware I'm doing something wrong."

The plan lasted for three weeks. I couldn't keep track of breaches, kids were tattling on each other, and the whole thing crumbled. We trashed the plan, but learned a couple of important things: one, the kids had a strong desire for healthy communication and were willing to be uncomfortable to make it better; and two, they were well aware when they acted in defiance of their contract.

We tried again. This time, I posted a chart on the wall titled, "WHAT'S THE GOOD WORD?" Under the title I wrote "KIND" in green and "CRITICAL" in red. I suggested that we categorize and tally our language habits and use this chart as a mindful tool—not to judge, just to bring further awareness to the number of kind things we'd say versus the number of critical things.

Two days later, my hands were stained in red Sharpie and the kids were saying things like, "Xavier just called me a toad! He gets a mark on the chart for that!"

I recycled the chart and decided to just let them be assholes to each other. Since I wasn't any good at keeping track of infractions and punishments anyway, we ditched negative discipline altogether and I told my brood that they would have to earn screen time through chores.

After a week, Penelope threw down the gauntlet: "I'm not cleaning for apps. I'd rather live in filth."

With another clever parenting trick failing me, I turned to God.

Fetal

While the kids were at school, I curled into fetal position and begged for a solution. "God, I feel like I'm living with little time bombs. How do I manage these personalities so I can have a peaceful home?"

"Go get a glass of water," a voice demanded. God usually speaks to me in feelings, so this verbal command in my head was surprising.

"I don't need water. I need help!"

"Water. Now. Go."

"I'll get the glass of water after I meditate. I just got into fetal. I'm comfortable."

"Go get the water, Vanessa!" the clearly-not-mine voice commanded.

"Damn it. Fine, God, or... whoever you are. Whatever, I'll go." I clicked my tongue and rolled to standing, poured myself a glass and guzzled. Wiping my mouth with my sleeve, I realized that I was dehydrated. Evidently, I was being my own teenager, resisting the loving, parent-ish voice in my head guiding me toward water because I thought I knew better. That's exactly what my what-do-you-know-you're-just-a-stupid-mom kids were doing to me!

I decided that perhaps it was time for me to cool my own inner adolescent before judging the ones I created.

With this tiny shift in perspective, I returned to fetal position. My brain begged and it needed and it churned and it problem-solved between meditative breaths for a good 20 minutes, then suddenly everything quieted.

Warmth rushed over and through me.

I felt whole.

"You don't need to *do* anything," a voice guided. Not my voice. Not really God's either. *Who is that?* "You only need to serve Source. Breathe in creation, breathe out service.

"Clever solutions are a waste of time. The charts, the rules, the power struggles... they are only necessary when there is an absence of spiritual integrity. Those constructs emerge from judgment... and judgment is a losing battle. Stop judging and you'll have a peaceful home."

In this relaxed and open state, this message resonated with me so deeply that it became part of me. I embodied the wisdom as part of my Truth. I stopped trying to manipulate situations by bending them toward my preferences and will, and instead just let the kids play out their emotions through their own free will. I stopped judging their fights, instead greeting each meltdown with one of my awesome superpowers: compassion. I dropped into my huge, juicy, compassionate heart space to deal with my babies, and even employed some Metta: *May I be present. May I be peaceful. May I hear. May I practice non-judgment.* It was like flipping a switch. The daily fights diminished to weekly fights. I could deal with weekly fights.

My kids are figuring out who they are right now. They are challenging authority and making messes because that's what humans this age do. If I continue to manipulate their growth to be in alignment with my human desires, I'll never know what beautiful shapes they could take as themselves, and they won't either. So instead I have to just hold space for them. When they say terrible things to me, I remember it's just the teenage years talking and work hard not to take their words personally. I try to ask questions. I call them out when they're nasty. I say things like, "I'm sorry you're so angry. Your words hurt my feelings." I hold my boundaries. If I am able, I hug them. If I'm not able, I tell them I'll hug them later. I respond with my other awesome superpower: forgiveness. I don't punish them anymore for saying things like, "I hate you," or, "You're a terrible parent." Those insults aren't my Truth so the words can't stick to me. I have a very different opinion of myself. The kids know that what they're saying is hurtful. They don't want to be bad. They're just stuck.

Do I still get mad? Yes. So mad. So fucking mad.

Do I stay mad? No. My forgiveness practice is man-eater.

Superpower

We parents must interact with children from the heart, not the head. Thoughts are not reliable. Words can fail us. The heart is strong enough to handle whatever challenges our teenagers throw at us. We also need to let the kids be who they are and express however they need to. They are not toddlers anymore. They don't need discipline. They need loving guidance.

Dropping into the heart is a practice, just like mindfulness. The two are close cousins. The brain generates and analyzes, the heart feels and radiates. Each produces a unique, meaningful response to adversity, but the head is hard, and thoughts bounce around in there, trapped. The heart, on the other hand, is soft. Thoughts that drop into the heart can take interesting shapes, be expressed fluidly through movement, and escape easily through soft layers. I'm finding that when it comes to parenting teenagers, the heart rules.

A week or two after this parenting revelation, I had a dream so real I could touch and feel it. In the dream, one of my girls engaged in phenomenally dangerous and inappropriate behavior. In the dream, I expressed my disappointment. I asked her how she could do that and admonished her for making a horrible choice. She looked at me with such deep shame in her face. At the time of her transgression, she thought she was doing something powerful and beautiful. My condemnation made her shrivel up and feel small. In the moment, I knew I was in a dream and that I was learning an important lesson. I never wanted to make her feel like that again. I knew that this lesson in non-judgment would become one of the most powerful of my parenthood.

I'm still living through this experience, so outcomes are a little unclear. But so far, all this Wonder Twin power and heart space stuff is working. Since consciously deciding to stop judging my children, my home has been a more peaceful place. Not perfect, but absolutely more peaceful.

My children did not change to bring about this peace, I did.

The relative peace will continue, so long as I approach parenting as I would any practice: as something that matures and changes as new insights are gained, and something that can be mastered with consistency over time.

This lesson is a repeat of a lesson I learned as a young mother: parenting books and disciplinary tricks won't magic away my problems. When I change the way I see the world, the world changes around me.

Closer

In their song "Closer to Fine," The Indigo Girls sing, "There's more than one answer to these questions/pointing me in a crooked line./And the less I seek my source for some definitive,/the closer I am to fine." There isn't one way to practice mindfulness or spiritually based mental health. In fact, you have permission to be wildly creative with your practice. Turn it this way, then that way. Shake it. Toss it in the air. Slow it down, then speed it up. Make mistakes and learn from them.

Your kids are here to teach you the most powerful lessons you will ever learn. If they don't vibe with these techniques or any of the ideas you're coming up with, let them teach you to practice peace through their innovative and wholesome play. Invite them to come up with ways that return your tribe to love. The discovery process takes time and may require frequent tweaking, but trust that the path you choose as a family is the right path—and stay on it.

I really do believe that there is hope for all of us through spiritually based mental health practice. My kids have responded positively to this shift toward conscious parenting, and together, we have created a sort-of-woke posse of our own. The emotional tone of our home has morphed from a frequent state of exasperation into an atmosphere of relative ease. Don't get me wrong—sometimes it's a legit circus around here; but generally speaking, we recover pretty quickly from the chaos. And I notice that those moments usually arise when *I'm* out of sorts.

The proof is in the pudding, so they say. Let me serve some up. One late afternoon two years ago, I was standing in my kitchen, chopping onions. Penelope appeared and wrapped her arms around my waist.

"Mom," she said, "I think I'm becoming aware. I was just walking down the stairs, thinking of all the mean things I wanted to say to you, and then I decided not to."

If she had walked into my space unaware of her energy, we likely would've begun fighting. Dinner may have burned. Tears may have shed. Heartbeats may have escalated. The other kids in the house may have been hurt by the drama. But instead, my daughter chose peace. Her self-awareness protected our entire family from a surge of anger, sadness, and cortisol production. If I were holding a football instead of a chef's knife, I would've spiked it on the floor. I wondered what could happen if more children welcomed awareness to their speech, knowing that this awareness would spare somebody 30 minutes, or perhaps 30 years, of suffering.

There's only one way to find out, and that's by teaching them. So, this is my message to you, momma: Your practice matters. Your examples matter. Your teachings matter. Your children, your

171

coworkers, and your friends may not be able to express themselves the way Penelope could, but trust that it's working. Look for the evidence. You will find it.

Chapter Summary:
May I practice non-judgment. May you practice non-judgment. May we practice non-judgment.

Rules and punishments are important parts of parenting but pale in comparison to practicing non-judgment. It was a superpower that I'd worked on for years, but never intentionally directed toward my children. Curling up in my fetal position meditation, I was able to understand non-judgment in a way that's hard to describe in words. There was actually much more to it than I could share in the book, so I'll tell you one day if you come see me talk somewhere. But basically, a part of my inner judge died that day. She was replaced by an empty breath. Clearing that layer of judgment created another tiny shift, not the shifting of a little divine cog, but of a huge cosmic wheel, and my family benefited greatly from the effort.

Journal Prompts:
- What usually happens in your house when kids misbehave? How do you react or respond? Do you want to disappear? Do you get involve? Do you judge?
- This week notice each time you judge your kids. Use a mindfulness tool if you need help remembering to notice. The amount of times you judge them will likely surprise you. Investigate the judgment. Is it based in your own insecurities? Is it based in concern for your children? Is it okay for your kids to make mistakes? Is it okay for them to royally fuck up? Are you okay with them being totally

different from you?

- Spend some time meditating at night then write down any words or messages that come from the most loving part of yourself. At the end of the week, puzzle together the pieces of your journal entries and come up with an internal covenant that helps you navigate any parenting issues you're bumping up against lately.

- Using what you've learned or relearned so far, sit down with your family and craft a family covenant. Remember that it is a living contract and will change over time.

- Here's a fun one: list your superpowers. Don't be humble.

Part 3

THEN...
WHOLE WORLD

20

May I live bravely. May you live bravely. May we live bravely.

Chosen

There's an old saying, "Hold the vision. Trust the process." When life hammers us with the shittiest possible outcomes—home foreclosures and pint-sized bullies, malignant tumors and miscarried babies—hold the vision. When husbands cheat and friends betray, zombies attack and skies pour acid rain, hold the vision. When we are worn threadbare and teeter at the edges of life's many chasms, we must hold the vision. **The vision is divine pursuit.** It's Chosen direction, not circumstantial direction. The vision is generated by the Love.

The process washing over us, through us, and past us is how the vision unfolds. Though we often do our best to avoid the process, somewhere buried within it is a lesson that our soul traveled all the way to Earth to learn.

Do you remember 2013? According to my new age-y friends, it was a total crap year for a lot of people. A mandatory year of karmic reckoning for us undergrad students of Earth School, 2013 was delivered with mostly unrequited Love by the cosmos. My family was included on the distribution list; we unwillingly accepted our yuck assignment.

I received this assignment while home with my brood, making dinner. I was stirring tomato sauce while the little ones traded

Pokémon cards on the floor behind me. Michael called, dropped a C-bomb, and had to hang up abruptly because he was driving and freaking out.

Yep. Cancer.

I turned toward the stovetop, secretly convulsing, retching, contorting, and trying my best to hide my panic from the others. *How do we tell the kids? Is chemo as bad as I think it is? Will he be in pain? What if he dies? The kids will grow up without a dad. How will I support our family? I have no special talents, no resume, no clear direction. I can't do this by myself. Oh God, oh God, oh God, HELP US!*

After a minute or two of internal nuclear meltdown, I promised myself a full-scale federal disaster later in private, and then engaged my mindfulness practice:

It's okay to be scared. Fear makes my jaw tight and my face twist and my belly ache and my heart pound and my chest heave, but it does not make dinner. Right NOW, I am cooking sauce. The kitchen smells like onions, garlic, and roasted tomatoes. I am stirring this pot. That's all. Right now, I am stirring this pot. My feet are on the ground, my muscles are relaxing, my fingers are wrapped gently around this wooden spoon, and my eyes are fixed on this pot. I am stirring. Just this. I am stirring this pot. Breathing. In through the nose, belly rises. Out through the nose, belly falls. In and out. Tears drying. Forehead smoothing. Just this. Just stirring this pot. Right now, I'm safe. Michael is safe. My family is safe. We are okay.

Before Michael's diagnosis, I lived in what I considered to be the peaceful valley. I remember wondering if my practice would sustain me if life took a tumble, even speculated on it, like a premonition, weeks earlier in my blog. I'd never had an opportunity to use my mindfulness practice in such a profound way. This experience proved that my practice had developed not only into a practical life tool, but also into a mature sense of acceptance and trust.

That night, when I was alone, I welcomed the meltdown, but it wouldn't come. It never came, in fact. While there were times when I felt angry, frustrated, or sensitive, distraught desperation never presented itself again. My mindfulness practice coached me comfortably through feelings in real time, with real perspective.

That said, I am so, so, so very human. The same pitfalls that challenged me before practicing mindfulness existed after I "turned pro," in fact more so while caring for three little kids and a cancer patient. I believe this is the part of the process that falls under the subheading, *Humility*.

A person under stress can only keep it together for so long. Eventually, something caves in. That's just what happened to me.

Caved

I'm naturally disorganized—I work overtime to appear otherwise. While my tribe was in crisis, the family calendar bit the dust. I forgot to bring my kids to birthday parties, no-showed for school meetings, spaced on outings with friends. I could no longer keep track of domestic staples. I lost keys, forgot to buy eggs, ignored stacks of mail.

At the time, I led Penelope's Brownie troop and Scarlett's Daisy troop. One April evening, the Daisies showed up at my house for a meeting, but the electricity had been shut off because I had forgotten to pay the bill. My BFF Julie shuttled nine first graders across the street to her house while I sat at home in the dark, begging NStar to come over and turn my lights back on.

There was a long list of humbling incidents like this over the months Michael was sick; but I hit rock bottom when, one July morning, I glimpsed metal on Penelope's teeth while she was laughing. I suddenly realized she was supposed to get her braces off the previous May. I stared into her mouth and bawled. And then I forgave myself, because sometimes life collapses in on itself and the kindest thing we can do is forgive.

Her braces came off the next week.

Scorched

If forgiveness is the number one survival tool, forward movement is number two. Winston Churchill said, "When you're going through hell keep going." I cannot tell you how many times I have repeated this sentence over the years.

Sometimes when you're in hell's fire, you become paralyzed. You learn to manage the current degree of heat you're standing in. You're like, *This is bad. I'm in pain, but I can deal. I'd like to be over there in that cool water, but there's a whole lotta unknown between here and there and it looks scary, so I'll just stay here. In hell. Burning. On fire. Ouch.*

In fear of the unknown that exists between you and relief, you avoid things like uncomfortable conversations, doctor appointments, cluttered basements, creeping rashes, expanding waistlines, dwindling bank accounts, and offers of help. You stay stuck. (Did I mention you're in hell? Burning? On fire? Ouch?)

The journey through hell, whatever your personal hell looks like, is not one to stroll through lackadaisically. Hell requires you to get focused, set your sights on a goal, and move your tushy. While you escape, you must pay extremely close attention to thoughts, feelings, physical sensations, and the landscape of your experiences for three reasons: 1) to avoid getting stuck there again; 2) to remember the way out if you do get stuck in hell again; and 3) to learn from the burn. (Our pain is not pointless!)

During my journey through hell, I consciously decided to trust the process that was unfolding, searching carefully for (maybe anticipating) potential life lessons and beneficial side effects of cancer. I was convinced that some good would result from Michael's extreme suffering. Having already withstood the hellfire of a disintegrating marriage for many years, I wondered silently if Michael's illness would somehow strengthen our union, a partnership that, over time, had come to feel more obligatory than loving. Perhaps cancer would change Michael or change me; together we'd suffer our way to karmic renewal and transform into two people ready to love each other authentically.

Surprised

I would soon learn that the "some good" born of suffering was delivered like anything else: through an uncomfortably long funnel of time, surrender, effort... and a hardy dose of holy-shit-when-and-how-is-this-thing-going-to-get-resolved patience. I would also learn the difference between *my* vision and *God's* vision.

Michael was actually diagnosed with two types of cancer: non-Hodgkin lymphoma and melanoma, both in early-ish stages, but still scary and shocking. A chronic optimist who embodied the power of positive thinking, Michael valiantly took on chemo and radiation. The idea was almost romantic in the beginning. My big, strong husband would bravely rock a bald head, eat veggie-infused smoothies, and take long naps outside on the patio. I'd take care of him and rub his back, feed him soup, and binge watch *Shameless* with him.

But this did not happen.

Instead, I saw sides of Michael that were foreign to me. I was bewildered. On top of the migraines and phenomenal bodily discomfort, he suffered paranoia, confusion, and depression. Who knew these were side effects of chemotherapy? Not us!

Cancer was not romantic. We did not lean into each other for support. The experience did not bring us closer together as a couple. Instead, the treatment served as a catalyst for our marital doom. For the months Michael's body received chemo, his thoughts, words, and behavior were all tainted by poison, which inspired him to stir up all sorts of rage-y conversations. I need to say, this was absolutely uncharacteristic of him. Generally speaking, Michael was (is) a peaceful guy, but chemical-induced crazies possessed him during that time. I understood what was happening and surprised myself time and time again by responding with composure to his rants and outbursts. *It's just the chemo talking*, I'd remind myself. I'd walk away, shuffle the kids outside, use my breath and my mindfulness practice to experience difficult feelings and restore equanimity.

But there was one day I couldn't.

The kids were downstairs watching Saturday morning cartoons while Michael and I were in our bedroom closet getting dressed. Michael decided he needed to understand exactly what was wrong with *us*, exactly what was in my head, exactly now. Sponge Bob's muffled laughing rose from the family room, the kids giggled while my belly squeezed. I remember saying that we shouldn't talk about this while he was fighting cancer because his mind was all fucked up from the chemo drugs. He kept pushing. Finally, I gave in. We argued. We said hurtful things. We admitted ugly truths. He accused me of being ice cold and mean. I accused him of wanting to *have* a wife without *being* a husband.

We went down in flames, right there in the closet.

Still dressed in my jammies and slippers, I ran outside, hopped in my truck, drove nowhere, sobbed relentlessly. My heart pumped, mind twisted. The rational part of me insisted on status quo—my marriage, my house, my vision. But another part of me was consumed by chaotic screams, *FUCK YOUR VISION, VANESSA! THIS FIGHT IS A GIFT TO YOU AND TO MICHAEL! EMBRACE IT AS OPPORTUNITY! THIS IS THE KIND OF PAIN THAT REQUIRES DIFFICULT ACTION! TAKE IT!*

The screaming part of me knew that our marriage was the thing really dying, not Michael. There was no longer beauty in our togetherness, no loving kindness between us, nothing blossoming in our future. We'd long ceased modeling a healthy relationship for our children. From a distance, maybe we could offer each other a functional love, but in a marriage, it had become impossible.

So, we did what lots of married couples do in a hopeless, love-lacking mess of a union: we stayed together.

Jonesed

In time, Michael recovered completely and earned a clean bill of health. His pleasant demeanor returned, and we went back to a marriage based on being a little bit mean to each other.

The cat was out of the bag, though. We'd let her loose that ominous weekend morning and there was no getting her back in. The thing that I'd known for years—that our marriage was unsustainable—was no longer a shapeless, contained, ignorable feeling. It was a clear thought: *this version of our relationship does not and will not work and therefore must end.*

The timing of this revelation was the absolute worst. In fall 2013, when Michael's hair was just starting to grow back in, he lost his job. In November, our beloved dog Rufus went into kidney failure; by winter, he died. Weeks later, I crashed my Ford. Cancer, unemployment, a dead dog, a broken-down truck, and a loveless marriage… we were officially living a George Jones song.

The great cosmic learning process of 2013 fucking sucked.

We continued trying to save the marriage on our own: mandatory weekly date nights, a weekend getaway to Denver, a KonMari bedroom. Each time we'd get ruffled by the idea of separation, we would smooth ourselves over, conspicuously ignoring this truth: *You can't convince yourself to love someone. Love isn't reasonable. Love isn't about want. Love isn't what's on paper. Love isn't material comfort.*

Love is a force that answers only to itself.

It's hard to believe we were still living together the summer of 2016, three years post cat release. During the time we dragged our feet, our lives continued to unravel spontaneously and in surprising ways. Another major car wreck, weird stuff with work, three weeks where every person in the house had multiple flu strains. I started thinking, *What's going to happen next? Will a piano drop on our heads? What does it take for us to wake up and realize our world is crumbling because we are resisting WHAT IS?*

The hardest part of separating was uttering the D-word out loud. In couple's therapy one night, boldness overtook me; I braved saying it. "Divorce" sliced through the air like a sword, hacking gruesomely through thick cords of security and commitment. With so many years and children and memories bonding us together, the suggestion felt almost criminal, but it also oozed with relief. Suddenly, a new path ripped open, one that was uncharted, scary, but radiating with relief.

This decision to separate wasn't for reasons personal or nefarious or offensive. It wasn't because I did something wrong or Michael did something wrong. The terms on which we drafted our soul contract no longer served. The union expired when we ceased to mutually benefit from each other.

It just was.

We exited the therapy session rattled. It's hard to describe the many feelings that pulsed through me in that moment. It was as if some old part of myself was purging through my throat. I'd been swallowing the word divorce for so long, trying to hide it from my children and my neighbors, it had festered and turned toxic. Saying it, decisively and out loud, released its chokehold on me. The air around me turned to fire and my body turned inside out. I gasped for breath and leaned into the wall, slid down onto the office steps, sobbed.

Michael responded with kindness. He waited at a safe distance while I slobbered artfully against the wall, said we'd be okay. "I've been through this before," he reminded me, an observation that increased the volume of my sobs.

Eventually I slunk to the sidewalk, looked up at the sky. The sun had changed position while we were uttering unspeakables inside. Late afternoon had become early evening in Porter Square, Cambridge. Thick clusters of commuters crowded the sidewalk, listening to podcasts on their ear buds, smiling at stopped cars from crosswalks. Michael and I wove between them silently, him a few steps ahead of me, far enough apart that no one we passed would think we'd been married for a dozen plus years. He suddenly seemed like a stranger to me. Unpredictable. Unreadable. The unsettling realization made me nervous and dumb. I didn't know who I was or what the hell I was doing. I observed carefully and tried not to invest too much in the thoughts and feelings. *It's just a feeling,* a loving voice inside my head assured. *It'll pass.*

Michael slowed his pace enough to offer me his profile and suggested dinner before heading home. It was a nice night, so we sat outside at a sidewalk café on Mass Ave. Over pizza and salad, we explored the most compassionate ways to break the news to our babies, then drove home to relieve the sitter, washing our faces with smiles to fool the kids a little while longer.

The scene felt strange and surreal. While they happily played Twister and baked brownies at home, their parents were out making a decision that would change their lives forever.

Yep. We were definitely in hell. Ouch.

Chapter Summary:
May I live bravely. May you live bravely. May we live bravely.

I share this story at this particular point in the book because divorce was my first and bravest step toward full alignment with my cosmic identity and toward creating emotional and energetic conditions necessary for my spiritual ascension. Had Michael and I stayed together, our unhappiness would have eventually been our ruin, and ruinous people don't ascend. I should add, this process is absolutely humbling; divorce is not for the faint of heart. If you have a spark of beauty left in your union, baby it, polish it up, and let it shine until it's bigger and brighter than ever before. But if you don't see any potential in your marriage, trust that you are worthy of happiness and seek it *immediately*. Don't drag it out. Your best life is waiting for you on the other side. It may be in the form of independence or new love. Either way, it's yours and it's liberating.

Learn that lesson, mamacita, the one you traveled all this way to earth to experience. The hell fire that paralyzes you is a tool that tells you three things: you're going through something hard; you have an opportunity to grow; and it's time to get your ass up, forgive yourself for wallowing, and move forward toward relief.

Journal Prompts:
- Hopefully you've never had to be on the receiving end of a cancer diagnosis, but statistically speaking, the chances are

very likely. If yes, how did the experience change you? Your relationships? Your experience of time or the need to use it differently?

- How do you react or respond to disturbing news or high stress situations? Do you think a mindfulness practice could help you manage emotions?

- Have you ever had a hellish experience? Describe it. How did you get through it? Was there anything you learned during the process that you've applied in other uncomfortable situations?

- A tiny little baby step in the direction of peace is a tiny little baby step further from the flames. Sometimes that baby step leads you through a hotter place, but if you're paying attention and you trust the process, you'll get through faster and with less scarring. Do you believe this to be true? Why or why not? Do you have examples of intentionally mitigated pain in your own life?

- Every couple goes through ups and downs. How do you deal with yours? Do you ignore things for a while? Nip it in the bud? Seek professional help? Work it out on your own? What works? What doesn't? Why and why not?

- What is your vision? Does it align with God's vision? Do you know what God's Vision for you is? What does ascension mean to you? Is it important? Why or why not? If you are not here to ascend, why are you here?

21

May I trust. May you trust. May we trust.

Woo-woo

I've healed so much, worked so hard, experienced so many lessons. To omit my personal story of ascension would be a disservice to you, to this book, and to this badass Sovereign hanging out inside of me. So, at the risk of losing you, I'm going share the "woo-woo" part of my story without apology and do my best to describe what the ongoing process of ascension looks and feels like from my perspective.

For many years, I could often be found sitting hunchbacked on the floor in the Metaphysical section at Barnes & Noble, hovering over texts on Buddhism, Numerology, Tantra, moon cycles, chakras, star children, Law of Attraction, quantum hypnosis… I'd buy anything that sent chills up my spine.

One day while rummaging through the Eastern Philosophy stacks, I was shocked to discover Jesus rummaging there with me. For reals. I closed my eyes for a minute, just to think, and saw him clear as day behind my eyelids. *Where did this guy come from??*

Considering myself less Christian and more Bu-curious (curious about Buddhism), I had never invited Jesus to join me for this exploration; I only invited *the Love.* But Jesus came along with the Love because, as it turned out, he *is* the Love. He seemed to trust me with his Love wholeheartedly, which, again, surprised me because I could be such a beast of a person and I hardly ever capitalized *his* or *he*.

A few weeks later, I felt his arms around me while I chanted in Tibetan at a local Buddhist center. Then one afternoon, while I was exploring past lives in hypnotic regression, he hugged me and told me he loved me. I felt his hot hands on mine during Reiki classes, his loving embrace during angel card sessions. I felt a calming presence that could only be his when I meditated on my family room couch, not always, but enough to know that this guy really wanted a piece of me.

Once while receiving acupuncture, Jesus lifted me out of my body and cradled me like a baby. My arms wrapped around his neck, my head rested on his chest, we spoke through our hearts.

Hold me, I pleaded.

I am holding you, Vanessa. I'm here, he assured. We stayed like that for a long time.

He moved to put me down and I squeezed his neck like a child would a parent, *Don't let me go.*

He laughed and held me a little longer before placing my subtle body back down on the table. I felt wanted, safe, indulged, and loved.

Just like Dorothy's ruby slippers, there he was and there he'd stay. During my weakest, most vulnerable moments, when I was about as cuddly as a crocodile, I'd close my eyes and Jesus would be waiting there behind my lashes, drenched in light, arms open wide, taking me in like a lonely baby bird, petting me and comforting me and loving me, welcoming me home to spirit, all patience and forgiveness, humility and assuredness.

He must have seen something in me that was precious and beautiful, something worth his attention. I wondered how he recognized that beauty so easily, when it was so hard for me to see it in myself. I wondered why he had such faith in me, even when I was not so sure about him.

Through the quiet wisdom of my practice, I came to realize Jesus was rooting for me not because I was special, but because he roots for all of us. *Come on, kids! You can do this. I know all that suffering is hard to feel your way through; but Trust me. Just TRUST ME. Happiness is yours today if you just open your heart. You are made to succeed, and this is the day you can do it!*

Yes

I define ascension as awakening and aligning with higher levels of consciousness. Having already shed restrictive layers of physical and emotional density, and having experienced temporary stretches of spiritual bliss, I felt ready to expand into new realms of consciousness and learn to sustain an awakened, divine connection.

Admittedly, I really struggled to do this on my own.

There are plenty of people who have been able to ascend through meditation or other practices, but for me, it just wasn't happening. I needed a golden ticket, and I found it through a new ascension energy modality called *Marconics*.

Though I grew up a godless heathen, Jesus's approval on my Marconics journey was important to me. Maybe it's because I live in a country built by people who insist on ignoring Jesus but call on him in every crisis. Maybe it's because Jesus had spent so much time walking me through my adult years. Either way, I thought he should have a say in our next step. When I felt ready to move forward in my soul's *ascension*, I knew that Jesus had my back no matter which path I chose.

Chapter Summary:

May I trust. May you trust. May we trust.

You know me pretty well now, friend. You know I'm mentally healthy. You know I'm committed to my spiritual evolution. And now you know I love Jesus. He's been tucked between lines throughout this book, encouraging me to believe in my capability to make hard decisions and do hard things.

Journal Prompts:
- Is there an Ascended Master you feel safe with? How do they show up for you?
- Does your current spiritual path offer you a viable path to ascension? What are this path's requirements to expand your consciousness? Are they reasonable action steps?

22

May I live all the way. May you live all the way. May we live all the way.

Befriended

You know as well as I do that life is nonlinear. Example: you think of your mom and a moment later she calls you, that type of thing. This is where my how-I-got-over-the-ascension-hump story becomes so nonlinear and jumbled, it's hard to tell chronologically.

Bear with me.

In the fall of 2015, my soul sister Denise and I opened Chrysalis Meditation Center, a neighborhood gathering place dedicated to spiritually based mental health, where we regularly invited talented local gurus to teach on a variety of topics that honored both spirit and science. One of our regular teachers introduced us to his friend Shanti who, at the time, was channeling something called *The Galactic Federation of Light*. She was like a human radio receiver. This federation used her voice and body to deliver messages here on Earth. Denise and I interviewed her on the phone to see if she'd be a good fit for Chrysalis. She spoke in first person using the pronoun "we." The words she delivered were so intensely loving and beautiful, so pure, so detached from ego, so commanding, so eloquent, so Christ-like, we knew they were not *of* her, but *through* her. I'd never heard anyone channel like that before and I got curious.

Shanti came to Chrysalis to work with a private group of spiritual seekers. We stood in a circle while she delivered each of us a targeted message. I waited my turn, patiently observing as she gently whispered divinity into awaiting faces. Some people received their messages and smiled. Others cried. She eventually approached me, planted her feet, rolled her shoulders back, and exhaled. Her brown eyes met my brown eyes. She smiled wide. "Friend," she beamed as her eyes fluttered and rolled back in her head. "You are our friend. Thank you for the work you are doing here to bridge the gap." She hugged me then moved onto the next person in the circle.

I was dumbstruck.

I wondered if I was part of some sort of intergalactic team.

Why do they call me their friend? Do they know me? Am I part of them? Like, am I the "we," too? If I'm doing work here that is important to them, is it by chance or by design? Whose design? Mine? Theirs? Ours?

I followed Shanti on social media and noticed that we were often working through the same spiritual ideas at the same time and with the same perspective. She recorded videos of herself sending virtual healing that raised the hair on my arms. She posted essays in which I recognized a shared Truth.

Basically, I was vibing with her.

Recalibrated

A year later, Shanti asked me if I wanted to have my *chakras*, or my spiritual body, "recalibrated" through a new ascension modality called Marconics. I said, "I don't know what the hell you're talking about, but I'm in."

She explained that Marconics is a collection of cosmic ascension protocols that operate at a high frequency, 144 hertz, to be exact. The treatment she suggested for me, a psychic surgery, would update my third dimensional chakra system to a fifth dimensional system. She would cut and uncap each chakra, releasing me from the karmic entrapment of my past lives here on Earth. The procedure would also reconnect me to a cosmic grid that would power my energetic body sustainably, sort of like converting a home from gas, which is limited in supply, to solar, which is unlimited in supply.

A month later, I went to Shanti's studio to receive this upgrade. Lying on her massage table, my body twitched and jolted as she administered protocols. At one point my left arm bent at the elbow and my hand and forearm lifted up, spun around, then flopped back down without me moving it. The involuntary wriggling and jerking puzzled and even embarrassed me, but I couldn't stop it. At another point, my subtle body peeled away from my physical body and puked over the right side of the table. I felt a dramatic elimination of deeply rooted yuck. Shanti assured me that these were appropriate responses to the treatment.

After the session, she said I'd be tired for a few days and that I would start receiving regular psychic downloads from my cosmic Marconics team, sort of like operating system updates on a smart phone. She said the energy work would catalyze my unresolved karma, moving experiential debris through my life at top speed. She also told me to be careful with my thoughts because I'd start manifesting things very quickly, and that I may experience the occasional unexplainable illnesses or spontaneous healing, but not to worry because it's all part of the ascension process.

Girlfriend, these things actually happened.

Manifested

Thanks to that energetic barf, I was left with a complete absence of fear, a major karmic windfall considering Michael and I had two homes up for sale and both were snoozing on the real estate market.

We were on multiple brinks and needed relief.

My friend, realtor, and fellow manifestor Nancy, who is one of many Earth angels you'll meet in this chapter, called me on June 22, 2016, "I was racking my brain on how to find your buyer. I made a call to an old corporate placement contact who has a family that will pay you a ton of money to rent your house, furnished, for one year. It's not a sale, but it's movement. The only hitch is they arrive a week from Saturday." That was 11 days away.

We jumped on it.

I immediately started looking for a house we could rent. All year I'd been saying I wanted a small house with a big yard on the water. On day three of our countdown, Nancy showed me a small house with a neat yard that abutted a huge park. A river flowed 30 yards from the back door. The street number was 77. My inner Numerologist was thrilled. We moved in five days later.

Michael and I moved forward with our separation but still had to live together, which was not easy. When we weren't avoiding each other, we were arguing about politics. I slept in Penelope's room. My spiritual practice, my babies, and my entrepreneurial passion kept me hopeful, grounded, and focused. I ramped up my meditation practice, spent a lot of restorative time in the yard with my kids, and worked on growing Chrysalis with Denise.

A year passed quickly, and the time came to move out of our rental by the river. Affordable homes in Winchester, our city-burb a few miles north of Boston, were scarce, so I found a fixer-upper 30 minutes away in a sleepy beach town called Swampscott. It meant leaving the town we'd lived in for 13 years, but the children and I craved the stability of a forever home—and perhaps safe distance from gossip—so we packed our bags and headed east to the Atlantic for a reset.

We bought a two-family house that was covered in peeling

black paint and topped with an orangey-red roof. It had choppy interior spaces and sagging floors, but the ceilings were high, and light poured in from every direction. The house was four blocks from the beach; the neighborhood's quaint streets were lined with front porch houses; I could smell ocean from the steps; and a steady stream of happy people and dogs strolled by all day.

Just in case there was any doubt about the rightness of this purchase, its Numerology[11] sealed the deal. I've been practicing Numerology for almost a decade and I still get excited when I encounter master numbers. For example, the Swampscott house number was 38 (3+8=11) and the acreage was .22. We closed on August 3 (8+3=11) for $605,000 (6+0+5=11). For me, this was confirmation that I was making a decision my spiritual team could get behind.

And there was more.

Directed

A few chapters back, I shared a story of unshackling myself from material burdens by way of yard sale. What I didn't say was that as I dragged my worldly goods onto the lawn, a parade of emergency vehicles screamed past my house. A local high school senior was in a terrible car accident a half mile up the road from me. He crashed into an oak tree and passed almost immediately. His name was Pat Gill. He was a much-loved human and his passing devastated the

---

[11]If you're not familiar with Numerology, think of it like astrology but with numbers instead of planets. Each number carries a unique emotional value and personal signature. Paying close attention to how and where they show up is like finding breadcrumbs dropped by the Universe. Numbers are calculated by adding all the digits in one sequence together until they are reduced to a single digit. Repetitive digits, like 11:11 on a clock, are significant because they imply cosmic mastery or intervention. Generally speaking, these "master numbers" are not reduced.

community. I didn't know him, just learned about his kindness through mutual friends and read about his achievements in the papers, but I was deeply affected by his story and his spirit.

When I was a little older than Pat, I experienced the very thick of my depression. I'd drive dangerously fast down country roads in search of large oak trees to smash into. I didn't want to die, just wanted to be dead. Pat's transition out of body was by accident, not by choice, but it carried out in the same way I'd imagined my own physical escape so many times. The parallel roused that immense sadness I'd experienced as a young woman. It was such a lonely and confusing time.

Pat's energy followed me, showed up in various ways: his initials in chalk on the sidewalk, his sports jersey numbers appearing in repetition, things like that. I did his Numerology, a powerful string of sevens (divinity), nines (karmic completion), and elevens (intuitive mastery). His numbers were similar to my own and showed me that he was and is here to help people ascend, an Earth angel for sure.

What do you want me to do, Pat? I asked silently.

I don't often hear voices—clairaudience is not among my psychic superpowers—but I received his answer loud and clear: *Get to work.*

Maybe my hard-earned, mindful perspective could help young people who suffer now like I suffered then, I ventured. Inspired by Pat's urging, I made some calls and started teaching meditation in the nearby schools, eventually partnering with Denise to open Chrysalis as a place where community members of all ages could explore spiritually based mental health practices.

Here comes a trippy synchronicity with Pat. Upon moving to the seaside post-separation, my chatty new neighbor Lisa bopped across the road and introduced herself to me, "Oh, I notice you have a Buddha statue in your front window. I thought it was a good sign. The woman who lived in the house next door to you also kept a Buddha in her front window. She taught meditation in the schools here in town and would read angel cards for ladies in the neighborhood."

My eyes wandered to the house next door—number 44, the number for angelic intervention. "Why did she move? Is she teaching somewhere else now?" I asked.

"No, actually she died suddenly… maybe a year ago… of natural causes… at home while she was taking a bath," Lisa reported.

I winced reactively. This was the other way I would often think about killing myself in my early twenties: by unnaturally slicing up my wrists and bleeding out in the tub. Lisa went on, "You could probably still Google her and read about the work she did here in town."

"I will do that for sure. What's her name?" I asked.

"Pat Gillbride."

I fell silent, turned away, exhaled.

Reconstructed

The confirmation made me all the more determined to continue my spiritual work—and to breathe life back into this house. Within weeks of moving in, I hired a construction team led by yet another Earth angel, Doug,[12] a not-quite-retired contractor who vowed with a wink that my renovation would be his last project before sailing away on his boat with his wife.

---

[12]There are some people you meet and some you recognize. Well, I recognized Doug, perhaps from a past life. He carried a major dad vibe for me, which was good because we spent enormous amounts of time together over many months of construction.

Doug and his careful team gutted that saggy black eyesore of a house to the studs. My kids and I lived there throughout the entire renovation. We squished our lives into three tiny third floor bedrooms while hammers banged and dust fell. We had to cover our mouths while climbing the stairs and wash our feet before tucking into bed at night; but the dirt and discomfort were worth it. Together, we redesigned the entire interior to make it a single-family home, painted the outside white, and transformed the ugliest house on the block into something downright dreamy. It brightened up the whole street.

I could almost hear Pat Gillbride cheering from her post in heaven, surely pulling cosmic strings to make everything come together neatly. She knew I'd do right by the property and more importantly by her beloved neighbors. In return, the house and the neighborhood took care of my babies and me while the dust of our reconstructed family life settled.

We lived simply by the ocean. In Winchester, I had hundreds of friends to occupy my time, but in Swampscott, I had just four. I was suddenly flush with quiet moments to heal, restore, and create. Daily activities included trips to the ice cream store and walks to the beach. I created a spiritually based mental health project called *The Grid* from my outdoor office, formerly the front porch swing. I played lots of Monopoly with the kids, got back into yoga, and even started dating.

There I was with my little fam, peaceful by the ocean, steadily building my career, when the realities of life in Swampscott began to weigh heavy. The kids missed their dad, who was still back in Winchester, and we all missed our enormous network of friends. I'd logged almost 20,000 miles on my car driving back and forth between the city and the beach, sometimes twice a day. To add to the weight, the home renovation slapped me with unforeseen expenses and sucked up all of my cash. I quickly grew tired of taking care of a big house by myself and wondered if home ownership was not conducive to single-momming.

I debated what to do for weeks, wallowed in confusion, made lists with titles like "Stay or Go" and "Pros and Cons." Finally, my beloved sister-girlfriend Alexis methodically helped me project out potential timelines and consequences until I could take confident action. **There is nothing like the freedom that comes with making a hard decision.**

Liberated

In April of 2018, I put my dream house on the market. It went under agreement with multiple bids in three days for $777,000 cash. My divorce was finalized in May. We moved back to Winchester in July and our timeline shifted again. An invisible puff of karma released. We'd lived in Swampscott for exactly 11 months.

My sweet, wise, stylish friend and realtor Kara helped me find a rental back in Winchester. I wanted a small, modern home. She overheard a conversation in her office about a recently renovated house coming up and got me the very first viewing appointment. They needed a steep deposit, which I wouldn't have until after my house closed, which would be too late.

"I could sell my engagement ring," I threw out to Kara.

She looked me dead in the eye, all confidence and compassion, "That ring isn't doing anything for you, Vanessa. Let it serve you now." I still have chills when I think of the way she addressed me, like she was channeling a goddess.

That week I brought my two-carat emerald cut diamond and platinum engagement ring to The Jewelry Exchange in Boston's Downtown Crossing. I told the man behind the counter I wanted $11,000 for it. He shot me a doubtful look and said *maybe* I'd get

$8,000. After a 10-minute consult with his boss, he came back to me smiling like the Cheshire cat, "How does $10,500 sound?"

Close enough, I thought with a smile.

Kara covered me for the difference. She'd just closed two deals and was flush. I promised to pay her back when I closed on Swampscott. "I know you're good for it," she winked like only an Earth angel can.

I got the house.

It was a pretty small place. I'd moved from 5,500 square feet in the big family house, to 2,500 square feet in the beach house. This place was 1,700 square feet. With each move another yard sale took place, another great purge. My possessions became fewer and fewer.

I *loved* it.

Less to take care of, less to clean, less to pay for, less to think about, less to distract me. As I shrank materially, I grew spiritually.

I stopped worrying about money, logistics, and resources. If there was something I wanted or needed, it came to me. Surprising deposits in my bank account, beautiful places to visit, friends to help me get things done... There must have been a thousand mini-miracles that took shape for me as a playful new rhythm took hold of my life.

I received it all with gratitude.

Chapter Summary:

> *May I live all the way. May you live all the way.*
> *May we live all the way*

This is a jam-packed chapter. I *almost* feel like I need to apologize for pummeling you with so many details, but I felt as if I needed to really show how the process unfolded, including the way I received signs and confirmations as I moved through it. The signs kept me curious, took the edge off the chaos. The process actually felt interesting to me.

Had this entire experience not been paved in divinity, I may have come back to Winchester with major regrets. But from the very beginning, I was guided to that house in Swampscott. Yes, I could kick myself for dragging my kids around Massachusetts' North Shore, but honestly, I have too much trust in this path to do that. My gut tells me that Marconics did what it was supposed to do: it sped up my experiences so I could squeeze a couple of decades' worth of pain and moving and messiness and faith and waiting and experience and drama and connections and achievement and losses and discoveries and completion and Earth angels into a tight package of 11 magnificent (and sometimes unstable as heck) months.

The moral of the story is summed up in the Metta phrase above. Live all the way. Don't stay stuck. Don't be afraid. Don't think you can't. Don't worry about what other people think. And as Mr. Rogers said, "Look for the helpers."

Journal Prompts:
- How does the Universe speak to you? Through cheeky winks or explosive signs? Write down some of your favorite stories of synchronicity.
- Do you have Earth angels that show up for you in times of need? Who are they? How do you acknowledge them?
- Have you ever wanted to take a huge risk? Move somewhere? Try something? Quit a job? Transfer schools? Did you? Why or why not? Do you ever think back and say, "What if?"
- How do you heal? Where do you go? What do you do? Who do you turn to?

23

May I live without apology. May you live without apology. May we live without apology.

Alive

During the summer and fall of 2018, I experienced a beautiful series of events that supported my desire to live in the light full time. On August 11, during the solar eclipse that directly followed *Lion's Gate*, an astrological event during which the sun and Earth align with Sirius (our spiritual star), I spontaneously ascended into a new level of consciousness.[13]

I opened my eyes that morning and felt… alive, high, deeply loving in a way I had only ever experienced while sitting in meditation. I was and still am able to maintain the vibration.

Mastery

The following Saturday, August 18, Scarlett and I hopped a plane to Marseille for a mother-daughter pilgrimage through Provence where we planned to trace the footsteps of Mary Magdalene.

The 11 days we spent backpacking in France were nothing short of luminous. We drove through lavender fields in a convertible Fiat, we went river canyoning in Les Gorges du Verdon, and we ate our

---

[13]I learned later that the *Lion's Gate* portal generates a high frequency energy that supports spiritual awakening and those who are ready can take advantage consciously or unconsciously.

weight in banana-Nutella crepes. One of my favorite days was spent hiking to Sainte Baume, a mountaintop grotto that served as home to Mary Magdalene for 33 years following Jesus's death.

Obviously, numbers are really important to me; they guide me. While we toured Provence, master numbers—11, 22, 33, 44 and so on, each with its own meaning and energy—beamed us from every direction. The day we visited the cave at Sainte Baume, we left early from our Airbnb in a little village called Moustiers-Sainte-Marie. We departed at 8:44am to drive 77 miles along route D22 with an estimated time of arrival of 11:22; found a shortcut and arrived early; entered the path at 11:11 surrounded by *les papillons*. (Vanessa means butterfly.) A single dragonfly, my sign that Jesus is near, buzzed toward us and hovered for a few seconds before flitting away. To add to the Numerological bonanza, we initially arrived in the country on Air France number 333 with plane tickets that cost me $1144, my rental car's license plate also ended in 44, and the day we climbed Sainte Baume was the 22nd of August.

Through the numbers, a spiritual language I understood fluently, Mary's teacher energy was urging me to take my *Metta Mom* show on the road. *You've got this, V-girl. You have mastery of your story.* I felt her coach, *Keep going! I'm here if you need me!*

Twitching

Scarlett and I finished our adventure with some truly incredible moments (and a beautiful revelation that I'll share in the next chapter). Words cannot describe the feelings of illumination, gratitude, support, and rhythm I felt during that trip.

Upon arrival home, I decided a few things: 1) if I don't get *Metta Mom* out, Mary Magdalene is going to be pissed at me; 2) it's time for me to take a more active role in assisting people with ascension; and 3) I'm really good at these mother-daughter spiritual adventures and need to help other moms do this with their girls.

Number three is something I'm still working on, but I jumped on one and two, rededicating myself into *Metta Mom,* a manuscript I'd been babying for five long years, and registering to become a Marconics practitioner, an ascension modality I trusted whole-heartedly.

A few weeks later, I arrived at practitioner training in Vermont. As the original Marconics founder took the stage, her higher self spoke through her human self. I closed my eyes to listen as Alison told a dramatic history of *lightworkers*, souls who volunteered to incarnate on Earth to raise the planet's vibration and help humankind ascend.

Tears poured from my eyes in buckets.

I recognized this as my own story. Somewhere in my DNA, this truth was all recorded, and as she spoke, those parts of myself revived. I started twitching, the kind of jerking motions I'd had on Shanti's table two years before, but bigger and weirder. Have you seen Elaine dance on *Seinfeld*? Yah. It was strange. I caught a fast, jolting movement from the corner of my eye. One of the program leaders sitting next to me was twitching, too. I was like, *What the hell is happening here?*

Alison's partner, Lisa, took the stage next, and with a lot of humor and realness told us "ascension symptoms" to look out for, such as spontaneously improving health and unexplainable illness. I thought about my last physical exam where I learned my thyroid had suddenly activated after 14 years of underperforming. The doctor even dropped my medication dose from 125 to 112 to 100 to 88 micromilligrams.

Then Lisa described an illness that felt worse than the flu but not quite as bad as ebola. She said doctors are unable to diagnose it, jokingly calling it "flubola." *Wait. What? OMG, I had flubola last week!* In fact, this mystery illness was so intense that I ended up in the emergency room, which is a place I will only go if I've broken a bone and sometimes not even then. The doctor tested me for a hundred things and came up empty, so I went home (against her orders). I woke up the next morning and felt totally fine.

I could write a list of synchronicities as long as my arm that served as confirmations I was in the right place, but there was an emotional resonance, too. The founders and their team exuded lightness, curiosity, and determination. They meant business for sure, but they delivered teachings with such levity and humor that we students could relax and laugh with them. It reminded me of the way His Holiness the Dalai Lama leads, and the way I try to parent. After a couple of days observing this high-vibing bunch of twitchers, I sort of fell in love.

The protocols for administering Marconics bodywork felt like a dance to me. Each step felt natural and right. Even though this was all new to me and I had a lot to learn, the techniques felt familiar.

Non-conformity

Through a string of divine growth experiences, I'd become so strong in my spiritual core, I felt certain that the Marconics path was conclusively safe and viable. It didn't change my religious affiliation or my lifestyle, it simply served as a practical ascension strategy that could, for lack of a better word, shoehorn my higher self into my physical body.

I drove home Sunday night, safe and connected under a sky full of bright stars, giddy about continuing my training in the months ahead, and excited to help my community get their bodies ready for ascension.

I know ascension strategies like Marconics may sound strange to a lot of people, but I can't hide this part of my story just because it does not fit into limited, conditioned ways of thinking. Society wants us to conform, but what if society has it all wrong? What if the world we've created is misguided and confused? For us to conform, we'd have to be mad.

Question what you know. Look closer at what you see. Gatauma Buddha said, "Doubt everything. Follow your own light."

This story is not about recruiting or sermonizing or even being right. It's not about comparing my burdens to your burdens or my methods to your methods. It's not about saying, *I'm safe and you're damned.* It's about finding viable ways to relieve ourselves of the density we carry, so that we may ride this gorgeous planet into the light. Your ascension path is as unique as you are, so have some fun blazing it.

A Course in Miracles says, "It is God's Will that He has but one Son. It is God's Will that His one Son is you." **You as in *you*.** You can't pretend you're insignificant any longer, can't pretend your effort doesn't matter, can't pretend the work is too hard or ascension is unattainable.

If I can do it, you can do it.

You must take care of yourself first, my sweet momma friend. You must get your head on straight. You must let go of heavy weights. You must discern your truth and be brave enough to follow it, without apology. You must find ways to smile.

Chapter Summary:

May I live without apology. May you live without apology. May we live without apology.

Next time you find yourself in a clutch of women yacking about youth soccer assignments and kitchen countertop choices, check in with yourself and see if the conversation thrills you. If not, it's time to start new conversations, perhaps about emotional vulnerability or life purpose or spiritual ascension. ("If you don't want to be at the party, just leave the party.") This is how we stay unstuck from the yuck and spread light into the world. We share our stories, we expose our curiosities, we take risks, and we follow what feels good… without apology and without asking permission.

I'm having so much fun on my ascension path. Some of the experiences I described over the last two chapters were challenging, many were absolutely joyful, all were interesting. I hope that my testimony demonstrates that there are lots of ways to skin a cat, but you can't skin it while it's still hissing in the bag. Freeing yourself of heavy issues allows all kinds of time and headspace to explore new ideas… new Universes. The Great Beyond exists for you now; it's waiting for you to get curious so it can reveal itself to you.

Journal Prompts:

- Where is God?
- Where are you? Just for fun, write down directions on how to find your house here on Earth, starting from the North Star.
- Do you believe in angels? What do they look like? What are they made of? How do they travel? Where do they live? Can you see them? Why not? Does that mean they're in a different dimension? What's a dimension? How many dimensions are there?
- How do you learn about the world? What is your belief system and what is it based on?
- How often do you think about stuff like this? All the time? Never? Do you ever talk about the cosmos with friends? Is it fun for you? Would you like to do that more?

24

May I be Sovereign. May you be Sovereign. May we be Sovereign.

Aloneness

Scarlett and I rounded out our French backpacking adventure with four days in Paris. We arrived at Gare du Nord by way of a gorgeous train ride from Avignon, then hustled across the city to meet dear friends for dinner near the Eiffel Tower. With full bellies and happy hearts, we strolled over to the skyward monument to get a good look at our favorite city from the very best vantage. We climbed to the second floor of the tower where we admired a spectacular full moon hanging low over the Parisian skyline.

As Scarlett wandered toward a historical exhibit on display, I looked down and noticed that I was standing above a message painted on the floor that read "PLACE TO KISS." The words were surrounded by a pink circle just big enough to fit two people in love. As I looked at that cozy circle, my heart flooded with aloneness and tears stung my eyes. I paused in that emotional space and felt into myself. I was surrounded and supported by loved ones and friends, so I wasn't lonely by any means.

I closed my eyes and stood very still.

Aloneness had a slightly different vibe than loneliness. There was something powerful in it, but also isolating. I took a full breath into my heart space and excavated deeper into the source of this flooding emotion. I saw myself standing in that circle, in the world's most romantic city, with no one to kiss, no one to love me *like that*... I love being in love. I love romance. (Hello, I'm a Scorpio.) Before me was a dreamy story that I could envision unfolding in magical ways; but I couldn't partake in that story because I was missing a romantic lead. I guess that was a little disappointing, but not worthy of this overwhelm of emotion I was experiencing.

I dug even deeper and found that the root of my aloneness was not in being single, but in no longer having someone to bear witness to my life.

Think of a small child, trying something for the first time or accomplishing a goal she's worked hard for. "Daddy, Daddy! Look at me! Look at me! Watch me!" she'd say. Even though I was all grown up, there was still a little girl inside me who wanted to be seen and appreciated by a man who loved me. For so many years, I'd felt secure knowing I had a partner to observe the process of my becoming and to shelter me in hard times. He was gone now. I was alone in the place to kiss, alone in my life.

Who would bear witness to my journey?

Vulnerability quickly gave way to a rush of chills up my legs and tingles at the crown of my head. With an easy smile, I remembered that I wasn't actually alone. God was watching me, loving me, and cheering for me.

But who would shelter me?

When I was younger and knew less of myself, Michael made me feel protected. Mistakenly, I thought protection was love. Perhaps we both thought that. Suddenly I knew differently. **Protection isn't love; love is protection.**

Crown

I know that love intimately now. I know exactly who was in that little circle with me: God embodied, my I AM, my *Sovereign*.

My physical body carries two energies that are unique, but both me. Vanessa is my personality energy. She's kooky and curious. She loves kids and dogs. She forgets to turn the laundry over and eats Junior Mints at the movies. The other energy is my highest self, my Sovereign, or what I call "Big V." That's my God energy— omniscient and bold, firm and kind. When in need of shelter, Big V comes forward, all confidence and *we've-got-this*.

You know that image of Krishna in which he opens his mouth and the whole Universe is hidden inside? That's the idea. He's him, but he also embodies something bigger than him. I understand this now, and not because I'm intellectualizing it. I know it because I embody it. I've evolved into my own Sovereign, taking complete responsibility for the world I create and embodying the world within me. This is the "whole world" the Dalai Lama urged us to cultivate.

I am my own protector, my own witness, my own creator. I no longer need those things from Michael, or anyone.

I hope you can hold out just a little while longer before tucking *Metta Mom* into a bookshelf or, better yet, handing it off to a friend. I'd like to explore Sovereignty with you. Sovereignty is the most peaceful and powerful experience I've had as a human and I'd love to share tag team perspective on it from Big V and me.

Know Your Truth. As the baby in my family, I'm used to being told what to do. I can't count how many times I've said these exact words: "Just tell me what to do and I'll do it." Relying on other people's directives taught me one thing: how to be enslaved.

Sovereigns don't wear shackles. We wear crowns.

For too long you have looked to others to discern your truth. You are coming to a point in your ascension process where that is no longer possible, not because the people you turn to are mal-intended, but because once you are Sovereign, your mind is the ultimate and only tool you need. Crystals, divination tools, psychic readings, shamans, priests… they were important parts of your journey. These devices and teachers helped you get to where you are now, but you cannot rely on that which is outside of yourself forever.

To ascend, you must go completely within, completely beyond. Everything you need is inside of you.

The most important thing to know is what makes you feel good and happy, and to follow that bliss. How does Truth resonate in your body? Make careful note of your "tells" and live into them. Do not waste any more of your precious time by betraying your Truth.

Quit the Comparisons. As I got further into the spiritual ascension process, I'd hear fellow seekers list a variety of third dimensional activities they could no longer tolerate. Some were: meat, pop music, guided meditations, and even sleep. With the exception of meat, I still enjoyed all of these things. I thought maybe I wasn't as "high" as them or perhaps I wasn't ready or worthy of ascension. After a few weeks of self-doubt, I was like, *Screw that.* Dancing to Prince and being guided in meditation are things that make me super happy at my core. So, I stopped comparing my choices to others' and slept like a baby.

Also, there were many times when I felt like I was intuitively deficient. The women and men in my ascension circle reported having daily conversations with archangels while I only had daily conversations with the mailman. They could see light beings where I just saw empty space. They spoke (sometimes boasted) of having telepathic abilities while inside my quiet mind, crickets chirped. Again, the comparisons made me feel inadequate until I remembered that I have my own superhero woo-woo gifts, like forgiving people *all the way*, like swatting my kids' knees from the front seat of a minivan *while driving inside the lines*, like Truth-twitching *like an Elaine-on-Seinfeld boss*.

Stop obsessively watching other people and craving their talents and achievements. You are not those people. The things they do may not be appropriate or healthy for you. If you observe another person's activity and feel confident that there is common ground, meaning you share aspects of Truth, then follow your intuition and adopt parts of their practice or lifestyle. If you see someone who is rising and feel jealous or desperate to get to where they are, create psychic distance between you and that person. Use their achievement as inspiration and remember to create a life suitable to your unique imprint. This is the only way forward.

Transcend Your Story. There's a line in Michael Jackson's song "Black or White," "I'm not gonna spend my life being a color." I love that line. He's like, *I could let the world set limits for me, or I could just be a transcendent badass and show the world exactly WHO I AM.*

I thought of this song while listening to a 2019 interview on NPR with Kamala Harris. Reporter Rachel Martin was probing for her intentions on running for U.S. President in 2020. Rachel asked if a woman could beat Donald Trump. Kamala's voice smiled as she remembered that the Democratic leadership in San Francisco didn't think the liberal city was ready for a woman of color when she ran for District Attorney. "I won," she said. "I won, because I didn't listen." Kamala Harris was bigger than her body, bigger than her gender, bigger than her skin, bigger than her perceived limitations, and certainly bigger than her doubters. She knew it. That was her Truth and she lived it all the way.

You are a powerful being—powerful beyond human measure. It's time to acknowledge that which is greater than your physical vessel and material circumstances and become the divine creator you are designed to be. You were born to manifest your desires through ingenuity and innovation. Your mission is to use this magic to bring your world to light. You are capable and you have permission. Do not make excuses that keep you in an outdated mentality. Let your greatness supersede your insecurity.

Captain Your Ship. For many years, I have had a habit of seeking approval from God. *Is this okay, God? Send me a sign. Is this meant to be? Am I making the right decision?* Through Sovereign eyes, I now see myself as complete and whole, with all of the tools I need to navigate my way through this human experience confidently and with tremendous joy.

Your soul is only able to exist inside your body because it was granted permission to do so by our Creator. That means you are worthy of being alive. That means you are here on God's approval. That means you have all the permission you'll ever need to live in whatever way you want to live.

God entrusted your soul with this human gift of free will. You do not have to turn to God, your spiritual team, Jesus, or any sentient being to exercise that free will. Your God-sanctioned soul captains the flesh and blood ship you're living in. You are an ambassador who's been granted full authority by the Almighty. Do what makes you feel happy—really happy, not bullshit happy. Experiment. Play in free will. Stop asking permission.

Chapter Summary:
> *May I live Sovereign. May you live Sovereign.*
> *May we live Sovereign.*

Big V's a badass, right?

There's a big difference between understanding the concept of Sovereignty and really *owning* it. In my personal journey, I spent years reading about other people's experiences of enlightenment, nirvana, and Sovereignty. I wanted so badly to experience it for myself. I think for many of those years, I simply wasn't ready to lift out of my density... clearly, because it wasn't happening. Once I was ready, I connected with an ascension modality that could help me lock Big V into place.

It's important to know that all spiritual modalities do not pass through or lead to the same places. There are a lot of pit stops between here and Source, so take the time to discern which method is best for you. Don't waste your time trying out dozens of different energy practices. Do some research, sit quietly with your options, and pay attention to which one speaks to your Truth. If you notice resistance to a particular modality, don't assume that practice is not your Truth. It could mean you're feeling a little scared, which is normal. Do look deeper into your resistance and label it, then scan your body for clear resonance from a place of security.

Now is the time.

Giddy-up.

Journal Prompts:

- Do you believe you have a higher self? Where is she? Is she somewhere out there? Inside of you? Where does she hang out? How do you call her forward? Does she ever speak through your mouth or pour through your fingertips? How does it feel?

- How do you recognize truth when you encounter it? Do you trust it? Has it ever steered you wrong? Why or why not? Give examples.

- Who do you watch? Is there someone in your circle that makes you feel jealous? Why? What are they doing? What are you doing?

Epilogue

Over the past decade, I've spent countless hours in pursuit of higher connection, curiously searching and desperately wanting, feeling disappointed with my inability to find bliss or reach nirvana, exploring ideas I didn't yet understand and writing about concepts I hadn't yet experienced. At times I felt like a phony. At times the little light I could conjure quickly faded.

Nevertheless, I persisted.

I persisted with mindfulness and experienced undeniable results. In time, with patience and surrender, my little light began to shine brighter and eventually, when I was ready, I was tapped awake and led to my path. Because of mindfulness, I was able to create enough space between my thoughts to discover new ways to heal, access peace, pivot toward hope, welcome positivity, feel more alive, develop psychic insight, feel into Source, understand high level spiritual teachings, integrate my higher self, love with an open hand, explore the world confidently through free will, and, yes, experience bliss. (Pretty much in that order.)

A thousand tiny shifts in consciousness swirled around me constantly for a decade and I did my best to write them all down. There were times during this process that I wanted to give up, times I needed a break, times I couldn't muster the energy to journal one more page of my complicated life journey, or maybe I just ran out of words. I trust that anything I missed is being recorded with great detail and accuracy in the Book of Life, and someday, when I'm whole again in the cosmos, I'll sit in the lap of my Creator like a child sits in the lap of her mother and flip through the pages of my sacred existence.

I look forward to that reunion.

When I was little girl, I was terrified of death, but now, in a healthy way, I welcome it. I have work to do here first, I know. I have children to raise and love to make, relationships to navigate and curiosities to explore, places to travel and foods to try, news to spread and souls to prepare.

There's a man who readies humans for ascension from his post outside of Fenway Park after Red Sox games. He wears a sandwich board that says something like: *Is your soul prepared for the end of the world? Jesus is the answer.* His intentions can only be good, but his one-man campaign is misguided because his message is too narrow. Jesus is the answer for *him.* That is *his* Truth. The only overarching Truth that covers all bases is *Love.* Because Jesus *is* Love, Mr. Apocalypse is on the right track. He just doesn't know that Buddha is also Love. Krishna is Love. Allah is Love. He is Love. And You are Love.

You are Love.

You are Love.

You must know that You are Love.

The end of the world is not imminent, but the end of the world as we know it *is here.* And *you* are the answer. Desmond Tutu says, "God doesn't have anyone else but you." The whole world relies on your willingness to wake up and be the light.

Each and every person on the planet captains a soul. Your job is to remember who you truly are, so that you can break up karmic congestion in your mind and body and detach from lifetimes of bullshit, creating space for the light of your soul to flow freely through you. Buddhists call the cycle of life and death *samsara*—it breaks open only through enlightenment. The planet is evolving and the time for mass enlightenment is here and now. It's not just for monks and meditators anymore. You are invited to participate. You can break through. You are worthy. You have the tools.

It's time to remember who you are.

You must begin to raise your vibration now.

You have become too comfortable with your density. And where has that comfort gotten you? To a place where you doubt your love for yourself? Where you doubt the existence of God? Where you opt for consumerism and competition and grudges over peace and collaboration and forgiveness? Where you stay hidden in your home with your things and your people and your screens and pretend you are unaffected by the suffering of others? Isolation, doubt, and fear are not *you*.

The obsessions with your image and your job and your grades and your advancement and your school and your alcohol and your gossip and your money and your winning and your shoes and your politics and your pain and your kids and your prescriptions and your diagnosis and your technology and your thighs and your convictions and your wrinkles and your decor and your hobbies and your past and your parents and your late payments and your complaining and your abs and your appointments and your reputation and your beauty products and your personal brand and your story and your rightness and your wrongness and your failure and your enemies and your fear… These things are not you; they are weights. They are density that you drag around all day, every day. You shoulder it, but for what? For other people? No. You shoulder it because the most fearful part of yourself is afraid to release it. *If I am not these things, who am I?*

The answer is Love.

The density you carry is like a storm cloud blocking the sun, casting shadows on everyone under its breadth. By breaking up the body's density, you create space for the real you to shine through. As dark clouds dispel, the whole planet benefits by having a wider view of the infinite sky.

You are the sky, not the clouds. The clouds cannot be depended upon. They are ever-changing and unpredictable. The sky, though, is constant. Confusing the two results in your delusion.

I have a long-time theory that God is blue. I believe that the sky was designed to be blue so that no matter where you are on this beautiful, dense planet, if you can open our eyes, you can see the sky and see God. God surrounds and supports you whether you remember or not, entering your body with every new breath, inviting you to rise and shine.

Awaken!

It is no accident that the pain of a pinch wakes a sleeping body. It is the same for awakening a sleeping soul. Your suffering calls to you: *Wake up! Wake up! Your time is now. You are an integral part of a divine collaboration that spans the multiverse. You must know that you matter. Your effort matters. Your kindness matters. Your forgiveness matters.*

Open yourself to the discomfort of evolution. Here at the very edge of your boundaries, you may find space and grow exponentially wiser. Here at the very edge of your human capacity, you may find there is more to you than you once believed.

Pinch yourself.

Sleep no more.

There's no more time. You must use your superpowers and heal yourself today. Begin this moment. Employ mindfulness practices to initiate the process of ascension. Work with some of the techniques mentioned in this book or create something unique but be sure to infuse your practice with meditation. Use this foundational practice to inform your ascension.

Meditation is the way.

Let me repeat this, because it is important. Meditation is the way. When you know yourself, you don't want to hurt yourself. When you know yourself, you don't want to hurt others. When you know yourself, there is space to wish even those who challenge you love, peace, ease, and protection. When you know yourself, you hear the one true voice that you can trust.

There is no more time. Your next breath is your invitation to ascend.

And you must not give up.

Healing is healing; all increments are equal in spiritual progression. Even if it's a tiny sliver of a thing that you have to put your glasses on to see, it's upward movement and that is something to be celebrated.

Because the management of mood and brood is fraught with emotion and intensity, mothers have countless opportunities to transmute suffering and lift out of the confines of the third dimensional illusion. Every head thrown back in laughter, every clean dinner plate, every 98.6°F, every immaculate countertop, every banana-shaped poop, every high five, every full night's sleep, every relaxed muscle in traffic, every silent car ride, every awkward sex talk, every "Thanks, Mom," every "One more push, Mom," every "I'm home, Mom," every gratitude list, every avoided hangover, every tear-stained yoga class, every *Hail-Mary-full-of-Grace*, every sweet failure, every sweaty jog, every try, every kiss, every breath—every one of these moments draws you closer to the One. It all matters and it all counts.

Understanding the undying, unwavering, unstoppable Love that lives in your heart allows you to see the very Same Love in the hearts of others. *You* have to understand first, though.

Now you become your happiness. Now you become your children's teacher. Now you become the loving neighbor. Now you become "… *whole world*! Hahaha."

Acknowledgments

You're probably curious about my own mother. Her name is Linda West and she is the most extraordinary woman I know. She is the person I call when I spill grape juice on the rug, when I find out I'm pregnant, when I'm thinking about cutting my hair short, when I'm searching for a yummy risotto recipe, when I want to brag about a job well done, when I can't live another day in my marriage, when I have a weird rash, when I forget my Grandpa's phone number, when I need to gripe about bills, when I'm bored, when I don't know how to make an ice cream cake, when I'm noodling new business ideas, when I schedule a breast tissue biopsy, when I meet a super sexy new guy, when I want to say *I love you*, and when I finally finish writing my first book and need an honest opinion. I tried to write her into this book, but once I started, I couldn't stop. To keep *Metta Mom* from being 600 pages long, I decided not to include her.

I am so lucky to have such a badass mom who is not only brilliant, selfless, and beautiful, but also has great taste in second husbands. My stepdad George West loved me when my own father wasn't capable. I could not have asked for a better stepfather. Together, my parents teach my kids and me the strength of human love and partnership by taking care of the Earth, its inhabitants, and each other with great love.

With so many people to thank, Michael, Chelsea, Penelope, Scarlett, and Xavier top the list. Together we rise, fam. Also at the top of this list is Chelsea's mom Nancy, who proved to me early on that Love has no boundaries. She welcomed me into her family with hope and patience, granting me full permission to love her baby girl. This is a brave, brave pack of humans—a family built and rebuilt on forgiveness, grit, hope, humor, and fearlessness. I'm so proud to be part of this brood. I cannot imagine how they must have felt watching me write feverishly for years, knowing they were main characters in my non-fiction tale.

I'm already anticipating a lot of, *That didn't happen like that! It happened like this!* I relied heavily on journals to recall details and feelings, but even so, truth is subjective. If memories are threads of perspective, then *Metta Mom* is tightly woven from mine.

Chatham Sullivan gave my grown-up love a happy place to land. He provides me daily doses of eye candy, obscure vocabulary words, and so much more. Ever a supporter of my work and writing, he's encouraged me to be bold and take risks in my magic making. When I completed the thousandth round of editing on *Metta Mom* and felt ready to publish, he convinced me to let him take one last look at it. Red pen in hand, he inked the manuscript until it looked like a crime scene. I hated him for it; I love him for it. *Thank you, bud.*

Jessica Curtis and Candace Coakley are not only kindred friends, but also the two best editors a *Metta Mom* could ask for. They've been choking down this book for years, helping me take it from a disorganized heap of journal entries and blog posts to a digestible flow of prescriptive stories. Their skill, patience, and insight are gifts to me.

My beautiful friend Aurora DeLuca is the photographer responsible for *Metta Mom*'s fun cover art. Her talent and vision consistently bring my projects together in a way that makes me look as bright as I feel.

I send thanks to Lisa Kogan for mentoring me when *Metta Mom* was a zygote. I was pretty sure I had something important to say but wasn't confident I had the chops. Her generous attention and humor-infused pep talks allowed me to see myself as more than just an amateur writer. Also sending much gratitude to Marisa Corvisiero who plucked my query letter out of a sea of solicitations at The Muse in 2017. Her belief in *Metta Mom* gave me the push I needed to focus hard and get this project published.

Early readers Gisele Gobes, Kathy Beck, and Mary Fiorentino, and full manuscript readers Jen Williams, Janell Burley-Hofmann, Kara Spelman, and Nancy Pallotta—I'm wildly grateful for their precious time, constructive feedback, and vigilant edits. My cosmic twin Susannah Baxley came through for me in the semi-final stages of editing with spot-on organizational advice that tightened up the flow of this book. Zyanya Avila Louis was the very last editor to touch this manuscript. Under the tightest of deadlines, she promised I could do the impossible. I cannot believe I banged this out. (Insert mind-blown emoji here.)

Thank you to Team Heaven—Gram, Pauline, Lolly, and my two Pats.

Vivi Reska, my little momma, could very possibly be the most alive woman alive. Her energy, vivacity, affection, and boundless love revived my motherhood day after day for seven years. Three cheers for hugs that make you know you're loved and endless bowls of rice and beans.

Kimberley Freund is my rock. The same goes for Mary Gobes, Denise Fiorentino, Alexis Gantsoudes, and Julie Sopp. These women are so much more than friends. They are my co-parents and my soul sisters. Our shared moments—phone calls, playdates, carpools, field trips, shared meals, laughs, yoga classes, sleepovers, fundraisers, walks, holidays, freezer aisle sidebars, gripe sessions, ski weekends, vacations, kid swaps, road trips, sob-fests, hospital visits, birthday parties, parenting classes, funerals, weddings, plane rides, backyard barbeques, *Game of Thrones* analyses, tennis matches, and spontaneous dance parties—are moments that make motherhood wicked fucking awesome.

I am so lucky to be aligned with supportive friends and family: Dina Windle, Melissa Cronin, Landy Gobes, Lynne Mazzoli, Patty Cronin, Anne Gobes, Peter Gobes, Denise Costello, Camay Kwong Pascucci, Becky and Steve Kuhlman, Chris Willard, Lauren L'Esperance, Tom Freund, Larisa Lindsay, Kim Savage, Sue Rock Tully, Laurel LaGatta, Nancy Tsang, Theresa Beach, Liz Arangio, Bahaa Fam, Sarah Malcolm, Hilary Binda and Kevin Dunn, Elizabeth and Rich Ganz, Christianne and Andrey Zarur, Cara and Doug Mehne, Andy Kelley, Linda Rakoff, Linda Tolentino, Janice Johnson, Pierre Garreaud, Tran Courtney, Jeff Shargel, Alexis Fox, Brian Russo, Shanti Arakumova, Alison David-Bird, Lisa Wilson, Carolina Avelleneda, Cliff Lee, Liz Mara, Julie Coulton, Joe Guarino, Brian and Shobana Albrecht, Margaret Lyon, Mary D'Alba, Madhavi Agarwal, Lisa Hayes, Elaine Anderson, Stephanie Visocchi, Elisa Jazan, Samantha Shanley, Leidi Rodriguez, my Cronin cousins, and The Willes. These special people have been here for me and/or my kids in various capacities throughout this journey of living, healing, and growing. I love each of them and am here for them, too.

Recommended Reading

Real Happiness, Sharon Salzburg

The Power of NOW, Eckhart Tolle

The Whole-Brain Child, Dan Siegel and Tina Payne Bryson

Making a Change for Good, Cheri Huber

Lunar Abundance, Ezzie Spencer

Many Lives, Many Masters, Brian L. Weiss

Mindfulness in Action, Chogyum Trungpa

Writing Down the Bones, Natalie Goldberg

The War of Art, Steven Pressfield

Judgment Detox, Gabby Bernstein

A Course in Miracles

Tantra, Osho

The Life-Changing Magic of Tidying Up, Marie Kondo

Peace is Every Breath, Thich Nhat Hanh

Buddhism for Mothers, Sarah Napthali

Growing Up Mindful, Christopher Willard

iRules: What Every Tech-Healthy Family Needs to Know about Selfies, Sexting, Gaming, and Growing up, Janell Burley Hofmann

Helping Your Kids Cope with Divorce the Sandcastles Way, M. Gary Neuman

Numerology, Hans DeCoz

The Three Waves of Volunteers, Dolores Canon

Astrophysics for People in a Hurry, Neil deGrasse Tyson

Marconics: The Human Upgrade, Alison David Bird and Lisa Wilson

♥ Connect with Vanessa on Facebook or Instagram @vanessa.linsey.

♥ Learn about Vanessa's fun projects and read more *Metta Mom* stories at vanessalinsey.com.